crafting
love

crafting *love*

sharing our hearts through *the* work *of* our hands

MAGGIE OMAN SHANNON

VIVA
EDITIONS

Published in the United States by Viva Editions, an imprint of Start Midnight, LLC, 101 Hudson Street, Thirty-Seventh Floor, Suite 3705, Jersey City, NJ 07302.

Printed in the United States.
Cover design: Scott Idleman/Blink
Cover photograph: iStock
Text design: Frank Wiedemann
Illustrations: Jill Turney
First Edition.
10 9 8 7 6 5 4 3 2 1

Trade paper ISBN: 978-1-63228-041-1
Ebook ISBN: 978-1-63228-050-3

Library of Congress Cataloging-in-Publication Data is available on file.

Lovingly dedicated to those in the world, known and unknown to me,
who build connection and craft beauty through their creative acts of love

Table of Contents

"Love is a canvas furnished by nature and embroidered by imagination."

—VOLTAIRE

"Love doesn't just sit there, like a stone; it has to be made, like bread, remade all the time, made new."

—URSULA K. LE GUIN

"In our life, there is a single color, as on an artist's palette, which provides the meaning of life and art. It is the color of love."

—MARC CHAGALL

Introduction

WHEN I WROTE THIS BOOK, I FOUND MYSELF THINKING ABOUT my mother, whose child I was; and my child, whose mother I am. I turned in this manuscript in May, after the first Mother's Day I celebrated without my mother, and as I wrote, I reflected on her for a number of reasons, including her relationship to crafting. When we think of someone who has crafted something for us as an expression of love, most often we probably think of our mothers and our children.

My mother was highly intelligent and held two master's degrees, but was not exactly what you would call "crafty." Still, I sift back through the years and remember all the things she tried her hand at: the decoupaged metal index-card boxes she made for Christmas one year (one of which I still have, adorned with a picture of Benjamin Bunny); the tiny trousseau of Barbie clothes she made for my doll—Barbie was born in 1957, just six months before me—including a little green-wool coat festooned with emerald rick-rack (which I don't still have, and would give anything for); the parade of decorative pillows she made for me—out of Kate Greenaway illustrated fabric and ribbon—when I was in high school; needlepoint projects backed in velvet, often Asian designs, that were both kept and given away to friends. She gardened and she cooked, and she was even the teacher for the Girl Scouts in my troop who wanted to earn their sewing badge (which we all did, after sewing an indigo jumper with drawstring collar, the first—and last—thing I ever sewed). Thinking back through this history, I admire her efforts, especially since I sense that they were perhaps more dutiful activities than devotional ones; my mother was not one of us who passionately *love* creating. Her favorite way of "losing herself"—or finding herself—was through reading books, and listening to classical music.

My daughter, on the other hand, has a wild creativity that both amuses me and inspires me. She makes origami stars, duct-tape wallets, display signs for her "store" (objects from her room she tries to sell back to her parents to raise a little cash). She knits scarves, designs original outfits out of unused fabric, constructs zip lines for her stuffed animals using her jump rope and an empty paper-towel tube bent into a triangle. For her, creating is fun and a natural extension of living. Anything is fair game as a material and as a subject. She is the person who gave me the most imaginative, and treasured, compliment I've ever received: at the bottom of a piece of paper on which she'd used crayons to color a yellow-orange sun, an aqua sky, and a pink, many-petaled bloom, she wrote: "You are my flower."

Both my mother, and my child, have "crafted love"—have made things and given them to me as an expression of their love for me. It is an exchange that is as old as time, the making of something for another, though in the last century—with all the advances of modern manufacturing—it appeared on its way out. "Store-bought" presents replaced handicrafts in many social circles, though that is a trend that is shifting yet again. In a fascinating, and evidently ground-breaking, study published in 2015 in the American Marketing Association's *Journal of Marketing*, titled "The Handmade Effect: What's Love Got to Do with It?", the authors found that handmade products are considered more desirable because they are perceived as being made with love, and thus literally infused with love—in other words: handmade products are seen as literally *containing* love.

It's an interesting yardstick to measure our art and crafts by—and love plays an intriguing role on a number of different levels: the love the craftsperson has for the craft, the love of the materials the craftsperson uses, the love the craftsperson has for the recipient (if known—but as you'll read in the "Love of Others" section, crafters can feel a love for the person receiving their crafts even if that person is completely unknown to them). It's hard to think of art, or a craft, being successfully rendered if the creator does not feel a love for *something*—activity, elements, or audience.

Five years ago, when I wrote *Crafting Calm: Projects and Practices for Creativity and Contemplation*, I did not set out to write a trilogy, but that is what the book launched. The publication of *Crafting Gratitude: Creating and Celebrating Our Blessings with Hands and Heart* is just one year ago, and this book, *Crafting Love*, follows. In some ways, this progression mirrors the experience of crafting. As we begin working with our hands, we feel a sense of peace, of calm; we feel grateful that we have a craft form we can lose ourselves in and express ourselves through. And, above all, we feel the love that is both the beginning and the end of our crafting efforts: love of our materials, love of our process, and love of those who will enjoy our work, whether known or unknown to us. Though the craft projects I've covered in these three books could be seen, respectively, as being more oriented to creating calm or expressing gratitude or demonstrating love, in fact every craft I've ever written about could be said to be doing all three of those things.

In a format similar to the previous two books, I have organized this one into seven sections with five different crafts in each. And, as with the previous two books, the crafts I've featured often don't have a lot of "how to" instruction. There's an important reason for that. Step-by-step, technique-laden tomes abound; it is my assumption that if a particular art form appeals to you, you will search out other books or resources that will help you to hone your ability to practice that craft. My purpose here is, and has always been, to inspire and launch your exploration—to give you a sampler plate of delicious ideas that can propel you into a deeper experience of whatever medium or meditation has inspired you. This is not meant to be a technical book that gives you detailed instruction; it is an inspirational idea book meant to get those wheels spinning! It is meant for all those who are creative in the way that spiritual teacher Osho described: "To be creative means to be in love with life. You can be creative only if you love life enough that you want to enhance its beauty, you want to bring a little more music to it, a little more poetry to it, a little more dance to it."

In the crafting of this book, there have been moments of love threaded throughout the process, like beads on a string. The deadline for this book came at a time when I was stretched both personally and professionally, but I was aware that if I could immerse myself in the feelings of love I have for this subject, for the people who you'll meet in these pages, and for this wonderful opportunity to encourage people to embrace their own inherent creativity, the process of writing this book around a full-time job and motherhood would be smoothed. One day, while doing research for this book, I spent a soul-nourishing afternoon in one of San Francisco's treasures, Green Apple

> "Love is the only force capable of transforming an enemy into a friend."
>
> —MARTIN LUTHER KING JR.

Books on Clement Street, which has a veritable labyrinth of bookshelves carrying used books and new, full of wonderful and sometimes unusual gems. As I was leaving the bookstore with some of these treasured finds, I spied a gumball machine promising "Literary Morsels and Bookish Surprises" for just two quarters. What I got for my fifty cents was a true delight—a tiny orange-red rubber monster, with a quotation from Maurice Sendak's *Where the Wild Things Are* wrapped around it that will commence this exploration and is my enthusiastic invitation for each reader here: " . . . let the wild rumpus start!"

Maggie Oman Shannon
San Francisco, California

CRAFTING LOVE:
ROMANCE

Chapter 1:

CRAFTING LOVE: ROMANCE

"The most wonderful of all things in life is the discovery of another human being with whom one's relationship has a growing depth, beauty and joy as the years increase. This inner progressiveness of love between two human beings is a most marvelous thing; it cannot be found by looking for it or by passionately wishing for it. It is a sort of divine accident, and the most wonderful of all things in life."

–HUGH WALPOLE

LOVE MAKES THE WORLD GO 'ROUND—WE LEARN THAT LESSON, if not the song, very early in life. Like the lyrics to the song suggest, when we think of love we usually think first of a love-*er*, the one "true" love who is destined just for us, our one-and-only Love.

Anyone who's ever been in the first throes of romantic love knows that it's an exalted—"rapturously excited" is how Dictionary.com listed one of their definitions of the word—state, and that all the starry-eyed, stomach-butterflied clichés about what it feels like are true. We see the object of our love as the most intelligent, capable, wondrous creature to ever cross our paths. Who wouldn't feel inspired by that feeling to craft something that lets our love know just how much we adore them?

With time, the bloom of romantic rapture turns to something else; our lover may no longer give us heart palpitations, but we experience the "inner progressiveness of love" that results in, as Hugh Walpole notes in the quotation above, "a growing depth, beauty and joy as the years increase." That full, mature flowering of love can also inspire us to create something for our beloved that shows him or her just how deeply they are appreciated.

In this section, you'll find ideas for showing both adoration and appreciation of your romantic partner. As we work on creating the fruits of our love, creating our lives together, it's important to let our significant other know they are still our #1, that we didn't stop when we said "I do," and that we still "do." Each of the five crafts that follow serves as a love note of sorts (and sometimes literally) to keep the embers of your romantic love stoked. Because that's the ultimate creative act, as Tom Robbins reminds us: "We waste time looking for the perfect lover, instead of creating the perfect love."

"A heart that reaches out with love
can heal a soul, and change a life."
—KIRAN SHAIKH

"I Love You Because . . ." Notebook

When we first meet our beloveds, they shine more brightly than they will with the passing of time. (Though the flash we're initially attracted to often transforms to sterling as we learn more about the characteristics we see tested—and proven—by life's challenges.) Whichever stage of romance you may be in, whether newly smitten or agreeably entrenched, there is nothing like creating a "I Love You Because . . ." Notebook (or scrapbook) to tangibly express your admiration and ardor.

I made one for my husband in the first year we were together, after we were engaged, and three months before our wedding. In a small notebook the size of my palm, with a cut-out window displaying a besotted woman with an outstretched arm and a halo made up of tiny hearts, I proclaimed all the reasons I loved him . . . and each reason was illustrated with an appropriate embellishment, usually colored stickers. Sadly, I used an adhesive (cautionary note: don't skimp on supplies—be sure you are using quality acid-free materials!) that no longer holds most of the little love-strips and has turned brownish over the years since it was made. But the sentiments covering both the deep and the surface qualities of my man are just as vibrant today as they were when I pasted them down:

I love the care with which you do things.
I love your love of learning.
I love the way you bring bath stuff for our vacations.

There were forty-two little "I love you's" in all. Looking back at this sixteen years after I made it for my husband, I see how my discoveries of who he was have deepened over the years.

While searching for this little notebook, I found another palm-sized book I had completely forgotten about. Thankfully, its purpose was scribed on the first page: "A Marital Record of Daily Appreciations Recorded by Scott Bruce Shannon and Maggie Oman Shannon Beginning on the First-Month Anniversary of Their Marriage." Flipping through, I saw things like "The way you hide the coffee getting into the *Notting Hill* movie" in his writing, followed by mine: "The fact that you enjoyed *Notting Hill* and that you're my leading man, now and always . . ."

This practice ended a month later. (One of the last entries: "I appreciate that you have written in this little book, every night in June, even though you didn't want to." Guess who wrote that one? Followed by "I appreciate your caring for the houseplants.") While it didn't last for us, it is a variation on the theme of a "I Love You Because . . ." Notebook that may work for you.

This is an easy craft to attempt, because there are so many love-themed journals on the market, and all you have to do is personalize the contents. Whether you make a stand-alone "I Love You Because . . ." Notebook or attempt an ongoing one that's a journal of your days, taking the time to express your love is important. Not only does it help your beloved during those times when he or she may be in need of a pick-me-up, but it will help *you* to remember the precious aspects of your partner that sometimes can be taken for granted.

Inner Inquiries for Journaling and Reflection

❋ Have I ever cataloged all the reasons why I love my sweetheart? What are the "big" things I love about my romantic partner (qualities, habits, behaviors) . . . and what are the quirky, little things I love?

❋ How can I keep the awareness of these many things I love about my partner before me? What little rituals can we institute to keep our love fueled?

"Only love is real."
—*A COURSE IN MIRACLES*, FOUNDATION
FOR INNER PEACE

EDIBLE LOVE NOTES

It's been said that "the way to a man's heart is through his stomach," which is, of course, also true for women. Having our beloved, whether male or female, cook for us can be one of the most romantic acts we experience—especially if that meal is crafted with love and the intention to bring pure pleasure to one's partner.

Not being much of a cook myself, I can't personally claim a lot of experience or success in this area. The only time I attempted it was to woo someone many years ago who expressed an interest in eating a traditional pound cake—a cake made with a pound of sugar, a pound of flour, a pound of butter, and a pound of eggs. Search now on the Internet and recipes for pound cake come up in a matter of nanoseconds. But at the time I was trying to impress my would-be lover, the World Wide Web was nonexistent; I had to go to a library to hunt down the recipe.

Long story short: I found a recipe, I made the cake, and he married someone else. Whether that was due to my lack of cooking skills or not, I'll never know. (I never tasted that cake, so for all I know it landed like a pound weight in his stomach!) I thank my lucky stars I eventually ended up with someone for whom "home cooking" describes ordering at a restaurant or for takeout, and is not expected of his mate. However, if cooking is an art form that brings you joy, consider not only preparing something for your loved one to eat, but also to *read*—make it an edible love note!

If you read the wonderful novel *Like Water for Chocolate* by Laura Esquivel or saw the film version, you will recall its suggestion that enfolding feelings of love into your cooking can have a tangible effect on its recipients. But one does not need to be a culinary whiz to leave a love note for a sweetheart that's good enough to eat—all you need is a little inspiration and an edible marker or food-writing pen. Yes, if you didn't know it already, you have more options than a plastic tip and bag of frosting for writing edible love notes. There are many kinds of food-coloring pens that you can use not only for writing your expression of love, but for illustrating them too!

What to write? Perhaps it is a bit corny, but it can be fun to use puns referring to whatever food item you're embellishing. A cake dotted with Reese's Pieces, for instance, could proclaim "I love you to pieces." Iced cookies flavored with mint could say "You were 'mint' to be mine!" Something studded with nuts could, of course, state "I'm nuts about you." Something honey-flavored might read "Your love is sweeter than honey." (And, of course, don't forget the possibilities of the little foil-covered chocolate drops that are known as "Kisses"!)

You get the idea—writing your sweet sentiments on a food item that can be eaten is a fun, and unexpected, way to show your sweetheart you care. As cartoonist (and philosopher) Charles Schulz once said, "All you need is love. But a little chocolate now and then doesn't hurt."

> "Love is the ability and willingness to allow those that you care for to be what they choose for themselves without any insistence that they satisfy you."
>
> —WAYNE DYER

Inner Inquiries for Journaling and Reflection

* Do I have any memories of someone making me a special meal or special dessert? What was the food item (or items)—and what did it feel like to be the recipient?

* If someone were to write me an edible love note, what would I want it to be written on, and what would it say?

Foods That Enhance Love

The power of certain foods to increase ardor or romantic feelings is legendary. Known as aphrodisiacs—from Aphrodite, the Greek goddess of love—the following foods might be perfect to use for your edible love note, or to serve whenever your love life needs some "spicing up"!

Arugula: This popular salad ingredient has been viewed as an aphrodisiac since the first century AD. It has minerals and antioxidants that prevent a loss of libido and is associated with fertility.

Asparagus: Feeding your love an asparagus spear may sound sensual at first, but to obtain the full aphrodisiac effects, it is said the ritual must be repeated for no less than three days.

Avocados: The shape of this fruit is what associates it with love, but it is also packed with nutrients such as vitamin E and protein to help sustain romantic ardor.

Bananas: Just by looking at it, you can probably guess why it's been seen as an aphrodisiac through the years. In India, bananas are offered to the gods of fertility. Some see the banana, not the apple, as being the original forbidden fruit.

Chili Peppers: Hot peppers have long been considered as a food promoting love. The capsaicin in peppers stimulates endorphins and, well, makes you hot!

Chocolate: It is said that Moctezuma II, the Aztec ruler, would drink copious cups of chocolate before visiting his two wives and many concubines. It may have been helpful: consuming chocolate releases neurotransmitters that arouse emotions we associate with being "in love."

Figs: Both associated with modesty (as in fig leaf) and fertility (as in fig seeds), this fruit is also viewed by some as the original forbidden fruit. D. H. Lawrence penned a sensual poem, titled "Figs," that compared them to a womb.

Ginger: Rumored to be a bedroom treat for long-ago French kings, ginger makes the list of aphrodisiacs for its ability to increase circulation.

Honey: According to some sources, in many cultures, weddings were celebrated with mead (a honey-based alcoholic beverage). After the ceremony, the newlyweds were given a month's (a "moon") supply of the drink, which supposedly enhanced fertility. Other reasons honey is considered an aphrodisiac are due to the quick burst of energy it provides and its origins from flower pollen.

Oysters: The aphrodisiac that usually comes first to people's lips is the oyster, which contains amino acids that trigger sex hormones. Legend has it that Casanova would eat up to fifty oysters per day to help maintain his status as the champion of lovers.

Pomegranates: Like the banana and fig, the pomegranate is thought by some to be the original forbidden fruit. With its multitude of ruby-red seeds and mythological associations, the fruit has long been considered a symbol of fertility. Pomegranates are considered a fertility booster because they support blood flow and are a noteworthy antioxidant.

Salmon: Packed with omega-3 fatty acids, protein, and vitamins that help to lift one's libido, salmon has been called a "sexual powerhouse."

Strawberries: Strawberries have been considered an aphrodisiac since the days of ancient Rome. The vitamins contained in this little red heart-shaped fruit help blood to keep flowing to all areas of the body.

PILLOW TALK

For obvious reasons, the bedroom is the place in our home that is most associated with our sweethearts. Feng Shui experts, in addition to suggesting décor that comes in pairs to reinforce your relationship, counsel that this room be kept free of any images other than the two of you. (In other words, no kid photos allowed!). Whether or not you follow that ancient system of environmental harmony, it makes sense to fill your bedroom with reminders of your love. One crafty way to do that is through your bedding—and your choice of project will depend upon your interests and skill level.

If you are a quilter, you might already know that quilts have historically been a way to tell a story about love. Some Amish quilts, for instance, document marriages and births; they are a record of significant events in a couple's life and stitched together with intention and love. The popular Double Wedding Ring quilt pattern is symbolic of romance and marriage. Both shapes and colors are chosen to document the message the quilter wants to convey. In addition to being a practical craft that one (or two) can hunker down under for warmth, quilts also are a treasured heirloom to pass on to future generations. I possess a quilt made by my grandmother's grandmother. Sadly, I don't know the circumstances behind its making, but I imagine that it must contain some message of love, given that it is intricately and obviously lovingly stitched from sweet pastel cloth pieces in creamy white and dusty rose.

The quilters among us may already be searching their fabric stash, ready to start on a full-size bed covering. Quilting may be beyond your skill level or exceed the time you can devote to a project. But there are ways to duplicate this idea of telling your love story through bedding that can be practiced by crafters of all levels. If (like me) you are among the sewing-challenged, why not start with a pillowcase?

Whether you make your own or buy a ready-made throw pillow cover or bed pillowcase, there are all kinds of ways you can document your love through embellishments. Patches, patterned ribbons, iron-on transfers, embroidery, and buttons in a variety of shapes can all be sewn onto a cover with a simple hand stitching. There are also many kinds of easy-to-use fabric paints and markers ranging from glittery to puffy and in all colors of the rainbow. Create a special piece that makes the "case" for your love—and give the term "pillow talk" a whole new meaning!

Inner Inquiries for Journaling and Reflection

    ✱ What are the elements of my special love story? Have I ever taken the time to document some of the things that make it so special to me?

    ✱ What words, colors, shapes, and symbols best symbolize my love story? If I were to distill it down to just a few ingredients, what would they be? If I were to distill it down to just a few words, what would they be?

EMBROIDERED LOVE LETTERS

It was on the website Etsy.com, probably around the time it was founded in 2005, that I first saw a listing offering personalized love letters embroidered on fabric for your beloved. Having been married just five years before, I was always on the lookout for creative ways to express my love to my husband, and I appreciated the idea that one could make such sentiments visible through craft.

Now, more than a decade later, a search on Etsy shows many variations on that theme, including a commission option for an embroidered piece that duplicates your own hand-writing. Should you have a lot to say, that might be a good choice. For those for whom brevity is the soul of wit (or witness), then you might consider embroidering your own love letter.

The "fields" upon which you work could range from a pocket to a pillow, a wall hanging to a handkerchief, and the only other supply you need is needle and embroidery thread. (An embroidery hoop is also recommended, for keeping your material taut as you work on it). What to say on your love letter? A simple "I love you" is always appropriate, but should you need more inspiration, there are plenty of examples to

be found. There are even lists of the "best" love letters ever written. The "winner" of one contest: Johnny Cash. On his wife's sixty-fifth birthday, he wrote:

> We get old and get used to each other. We think alike. We read each others [sic] minds. We know what the other wants without asking. Sometimes we irritate each other a little bit. Maybe sometimes take each other for granted.
>
> But once in a while, like today, I meditate on it and realize how lucky I am to share my life with the greatest woman I ever met. You still fascinate and inspire me. You influence me for the better. You're the object of my desire, the #1 Earthly reason for my existence. I love you very much.

Now imagine those words embroidered on a piece of fabric—something that could be looked at or even carried every day. *That* is a gift that keeps on giving . . . and as Mother Teresa once said, "If you want a love message to be heard, it has to be sent out."

Inner Inquiries for Journaling and Reflection

* Have I ever written my beloved a love letter? If so, when was the last time I did?

* What is the message I would most want my beloved to hear on a daily basis? What is the message I would most want to hear from my beloved on a daily basis?

BUCKET LIST

The French novelist Antoine de Saint-Exupery penned a phrase often found on anniversary cards: "Love does not consist in gazing at each other, but in looking outward together in the same direction." As every long-time lover knows, the "gazing at each other" stage only lasts so long; the glue that keeps people bonded is sharing the same vision for life.

Should this be the phase you find yourself in, celebrate your relationship's maturity by crafting an expression of that common vision in the form of a bucket list. Not a list of things you want to do before you die, but a *literal* "list" in a bucket. Buckets in many sizes and made of an array of material abound in craft shops and dollar stores. Finding the right container for this craft is the first step. Decide what you want your bucket list to focus on—date-night ideas? Trips to take? Goals to achieve together? This focus will dictate the size of bucket you choose. Bigger bucket, bigger (or longer) focus. You can buy buckets already painted a particular color or design or paint or decoupage your own. You can use a permanent-ink pen to write phrases on your bucket; you can embellish it with any theme-appropriate charms or ribbons that you find.

Then, fill your bucket! Use special paper, such as origami paper cut into strips, or colored paper—anything that lights you up when looking inside your bucket—to write down all the ideas, suggestions and hopes for your particular bucket list. Decide the ritual you'll use with your partner in both filling it and choosing from it. Will you each take turns writing down ideas for a date and take turns choosing a slip? Is your bucket for suggesting ways in which you'd like your lover to attend to you (or vice versa), and you each select one every week? If your bucket contains goals you share, will you take one slip out on New Year's Eve to focus on in the new year?

> "Practice love until you remember that you are love."
>
> —SWAMI SAI PREMANANDA

The possibilities for jointly working with your bucket list are as varied as the possible themes for it. But having a vehicle in place, particularly a fun one such as this, can be helpful for keeping your relationship's intentions right in front of you. You will be following the good guidance of American poet Sam Walter Foss, who wrote: "See not for fresher founts afar, just drop your bucket where you are."

Inner Inquiries for Journaling and Reflection

* What is on my personal "bucket list"? Is this something that I can incorporate into my relationship, or is it strictly a personal goal?

* What would I like to experience with my beloved? At the end of life, what are the things that I will feel grateful for having done with him or her?

Love you

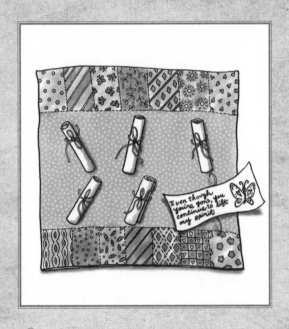

Even though you're gone, you continue to lift my spirit

CRAFTING LOVE:
FRIENDS/TEACHERS/MENTORS

Chapter 2:

CRAFTING LOVE:
FRIENDS/TEACHERS/MENTORS

> "You don't get to pick your family, but you can pick your teachers and you can pick
> your friends and you can pick the music you listen to and you can pick the books
> you read and you can pick the movies you see. You are, in fact, a mashup of what
> you choose to let into your life. You are the sum of your influences. The German
> writer Goethe said, 'We are shaped and fashioned by what we love.' "
> —AUSTIN KLEON

FOR MANY PEOPLE, ONE'S FAMILY OF ORIGIN CAN BE A challenging group to truly feel at home in, but when it comes to our friends, teachers and mentors—as Austin Kleon points out—we have chosen to let them into our lives. For that reason, they play just as important a role in our histories—sometimes, in fact, an even more important role. Modern personal-growth guru Jim Rohn has warned that "you are the average of the five people you spend the most time with." Motivational speaker Steve Maraboli has put it more directly: "If you hang out with chickens, you're going to cluck and if you hang out with eagles, you're going to fly."

This section is dedicated to the eagles—those friends, teachers, and mentors who have helped us to fly. Too often we forget to take the time to let them know how much they mean to us, or we erroneously assume that they just somehow *know*. But even if they do have an inkling of the important role they play in our lives, why not tangibly express your gratitude and love through one of the following creative expressions? Don't give them something to cluck about—thank the eagles in your life for giving you wings.

> "No one is born hating another person because of the color of his skin, or his background, or his religion. People must learn to hate, and if they can learn to hate, they can be taught to love, for love comes more naturally to the human heart than its opposite."
>
> —NELSON MANDELA

FRIENDSHIP BEADS

If you look at the cover of this book, you will see something very similar to the beautiful friendship necklace my friend Molly Starr made for me. It has been under my computer screen as I've written this, serving as both an inspiration and a literal touchstone of inspiration along the way. Seven beautiful, flat oval turquoise stones—each different, ranging in color from sky blue to deep teal—are the centerpiece of the necklace, separated by silver spacer beads in the form of a spiral circle. Molly—who is my best friend, was my matron of honor, and who is now my child's godmother—explains how she started making friendship necklaces as a spiritual practice and as an expression of love:

> My art began as beaded jewelry for myself. I'm afraid it was largely ego-based vanity, to display beautiful, sparkling creations, mostly crystal and pearls. Then I donated some pieces to the annual fundraising gala for San Francisco's Stepping Stone, a recovery home for working women. Initially I found it a challenge to let go of what I had made, especially as I realized that I could remember what I was watching or listening to as I made each piece. I would pick up the necklace or bracelet and as I touched it, the music playing as I worked, the view of the bay that day, and the words I spoke to myself as I made it all came back to me. I became lost in my five senses as I crafted. That was the turning point. For the last three years, I have put intent into

each item, bead, or piece I was stringing. Each piece is a creation of love and specific purpose—no longer just jewelry, but sacred art.

Two examples of my current spiritual process are the turquoise and silver JOY necklace I made for you on your birthday [described above]; and the SOLACE bracelet I made for another friend who was going through a deep grieving period. For yours, each turquoise oval bead was blessed with a joyous memory of our friendship, and the silver pieces on the necklace represent safety and stability in your life. The background music playing as I made the necklace was from the Buena Vista Social Club!

The grief bracelet I made consisted of six tiny gold and crystal beads representing my prayers for my friend's spiritual strength and were separated by slightly larger gold cloisonné beads which symbolized the momentary release of her grief burden. In other words, six steps to turning it over! The background music when I made this was from Loreena McKennitt. My friend used it as a rosary, touching the little beads to pray for grace and gratitude and the larger one to feel a moment of peace and freedom. She said it helped.

If you are drawn to the idea of making friendship jewelry to express your love for a treasured chum, Molly counsels that the materials used be chosen carefully:

My advice is to be very careful what materials you select for your art. I find that certain materials speak to me. I was drawn recently to colorful recycled glass and knew for me they represented eternal grace. It's an opportunity for me to hone my spiritual practice over and over, seeking the divine connection.

I no longer make jewelry just as decorative art. For me, it is important to make specific pieces for real-life people and situations—such as a bracelet for a bride signifying clear communication between partners and with the Divine.

For Molly, these beads are a literal representation of the thoughtful depth of her friendships . . . and remind me of painter Vincent van Gogh's wonderful words: "I feel there is nothing more truly artistic than to love people."

Inner Inquiries for Journaling and Reflection

* Do I include any other elements—such as Molly's musical soundtracks—into my creating time? What distinguishes my "decorative art" from my sacred art?

* If I could distill my feelings or intentions for my friend into just a few words, what would they be? What shapes, colors, or patterns could I use to convey that?

The Properties of Gemstones

Since I just wrote about the beautiful turquoise necklace that my dear friend Molly made for me, and knew that a turquoise bead strand would be used for the cover of this book, I was intrigued to discover that the lore surrounding turquoise includes friendship. Turquoise has traditionally been credited with the property of enhancing the bond between kindred spirits, as noted in a traditional saying that "he, or she, who owns a turquoise will never want for a friend."

If you would like to express your love for a special friend, teacher or mentor by using stone beads, here are some common associations:

Amber: While amber is considered a helpful stone for romantic love and marriage, it also is a good "general" love stone, associated with purification (drawing out negativity), protection, clarity, and calm.

Emerald: Though emerald is another stone associated with romance, it also is seen as a friendship stone and one that can bring balance to relationships. It is said to cultivate inspiration and patience, and to be helpful with communication and truthful expression.

Garnet: Considered a protection stone, garnet is said to bring forth abundance and other positive manifestations, including stability and career success.

Jade: Jade comes in several colors, but deep green stones (the color of the heart chakra) are the most valued. Jade is seen as a heart stone, good for all types of love. It is associated with serenity, generosity, and faithfulness in relationships.

Moonstone: Moonstone is also associated with all types of love, and is considered to be a good stone for enhancing a sense of hopefulness and calm. Seen as a stone of protection, moonstone is also associated with intuitive and psychic abilities.

Rose Quartz: Rose quartz *is* the "love stone," the stone that, above all others, is seen as enhancing any form of love—self-love, platonic love, and romantic love. It is also sometimes used when people are making the transition from life to death, to gently ease that process toward Divine Love.

Ruby: While ruby has been used as a stone to stoke passionate love, it is seen as being helpful in other settings as well—including heightening courage, inner strength, prosperity, and self-confidence.

Topaz: Topaz is the "spiritual love" stone. It is said to balance emotions, enhance creativity, and to bring feelings of hope and peace.

Turquoise: As mentioned above, turquoise is a symbol of friendship. If turquoise is given to another by a friend, it is said to both bring good luck and to dispel negative energy.

COOKIES AND POEMS

It's not easy to create a feeling of community in a place that sees 2,500 vendors and 20,000 buyers come through its doors every month, but Joan Rivard has done exactly that at the Rose Bowl Flea Market in Pasadena, California, which she calls the "swap meet." For more than 20 years, Joan has been using two forms of expressing love—making cookies with hearts on them and writing her heart-felt printed poems—to create bonds with regulars she now sees as being more than friends. They have become a sort of tribe.

Known as "The Cookie Lady," Joan sells homemade cookies (raspberry shortbread, pecan shortbread, or oatmeal raisin, all adorned with edible hearts) for just one dollar— although she gives away as many as she sells. She's not a vendor herself. Joan has come to be a part of the Flea Market with her consistent presence there for more than two decades, and has been told by others that it's just not the swap meet until she's there!

Joan talks about her metamorphosis into The Cookie Lady: "I wear . . . well, it's not a costume exactly, it's more a form of signifying what I believe in and what I'm going through. I wear 'hippie clothes'—I have a heaven-blue long skirt, a rainbow ribbon belt, a special hat that is wide-brimmed with purple flowers and has a rainbow ribbon to tie under my chin. All of the pieces I wear have been given to me." As The Cookie Lady, she goes up and down the aisles, seeking out old friends and making new ones. "Someone told me that I'm a legend here!" Joan reports.

But The Cookie Lady is known for more than her cookies—she also has given away thousands of her poems, both to people who buy her cookies and to strangers. Her poems detail the warm experience she feels at the flea market. She describes it as being almost transcendent: "I feel the presence of God really strong in these people . . . I get really high on it. The poetry seems like it comes from beyond myself. I love these people—they're like family." Here are excerpts from Joan's poem about her experience creating family from friends met at the swap meet:

SWAP MEET V: THE COOKIE LADY

Brotherly love is what she saw among the vendors and the customers,
the kind that can heal worlds and fix the laws.
She said that they were all shining with light and that was why
she couldn't tell them apart, because all of them looked like God.

At the swap meet, in the golden sunlight, she soaked up people's light
and radiated it back.
She drank in the strength and wisdom from each face,
which seemed to truly glow, transfigured in the natural light. Moving through crowds,
swimming through seas of people, she saw in everyone a holy light . . .
She often didn't sell all her cookies, moving too slow for real commerce to succeed,
having such a good time she didn't care.

What the vendors gave her was so much more than crumpled bills stuffed in her pouch.
Seeing their smiles she felt that she encountered the Divine.
The people seemed to her to glow as the sun set,
catching the fine hair on their skin with an ethereal light.
The vendors looked like angels taking down their booths

and skillfully loading their trucks,
giving each other hugs and good wishes till the next show.
They asked each other about their day, fibbed to each other
about how young they looked.
No matter how tired they were, some said they felt strangely refreshed.
Lifting up boxes and old furniture they seemed to her like Atlas lifting up the world,
exchanging smiles that could light up the parking lot if it weren't day.

Though Joan says she does not possess a lot of money, she'll have up to five hundred copies of her poems printed up, double-sided, in order to spread her poetic love for free. "People come back to me and say they cried when they read it," Joan says. "Our actual families don't always understand, but the people who come say I describe what the swap meet is like—I feel like I make them into a family."

For Joan, expressing love (and inspiring love) through the work of her hands and heart has created a community, an identity, and a calling—Joan hopes to find other ways to connect people who are interested in coming together; and her current dream is to start a movement for people to meet their neighbors at potluck parties in their neighborhoods the first Saturday of the month. Using your art to craft relationships—that is delicious stuff, indeed.

Inner Inquiries for Journaling and Reflection

✳ Do I have any creative expressions that I give out for free? If not, what would I be willing to give out for free?

✳ Do I have any communities in my life that feel like family to me? If not, what kind of community would I like to be a part of?

CLOTH TOTEMS

I can't remember when or how I was first introduced to the technique of transferring photographs to unbleached muslin, resulting in a cloth version of one's favorite picture. But I do remember that for a time in my twenties I was eagerly canvassing every printed image that came my way for its creative possibilities as a cloth pillow or art doll.

I had completely forgotten about one of these photographic forays onto fabric until my friend Beth reminded me that at the height of this creative compulsion, I had made a cloth image of someone who had been a source of inspiration since I was a teenager—and who still inspires me, in many ways: the singer/songwriter Bruce Springsteen. It amuses (and somewhat embarrasses) me now to think about it, but yes, I did find a large image of The Boss that I transferred onto muslin to make a . . . pillow? Doll? Totem? I'm not sure what you'd call it, but I cop to the act.

This was not fueled by any kind of weird fan obsession (though I have always thought he is kind of cute), but by wanting to surround myself with a source of inspiration and energy. Talk about "crafting love"—as anyone knows who has ever seen Springsteen in concert, the complete and pure joy he still exhibits in performance while in the flow of his artistic expression is what I wanted this figure to remind me of. It was a reminder that by stepping into your creative passion, you inspire that passion in others.

If you, too, either have a real-life person who inspires you—someone in your life, such as a special friend, teacher or mentor, or a public figure who inspires you in some way—or if you are drawn to some other representation of an admired quality, such as a favorite character in a book or movie, then you might consider making a cloth totem to remind you of their special attributes, as I did. After all, everyone needs remembrances to help us, in the words of Bruce, to "show a little faith . . . there's magic in the night!"

Since the possibilities for the subject of your cloth totem are, of course, as wide as the territory of your heart, so are the ways we use it. You might want to give your cloth totem of a special friend to that person, to let them know how much you love and appreciate him or her. You might simply want to make a representation of someone who inspires you, as I did with my Springsteen totem. They can, of course, represent people who are still living, or not. (One could make a series of cloth totems of women throughout history, for instance, whose examples stir you.) Or your cloth totem could represent qualities you hope to embody, and not signify an actual person at all. (Think of arresting images in advertising.) What you are exploring with this activity is whatever (or whoever) touches your heart, and inspires you, impresses you, enlivens you—because Baby, we *were* born to run.

Inner Inquiries for Journaling and Reflection

✳ Who in my life—either known personally or known about—inspires me in some way? What qualities do they have that make me feel inspired?

✳ What would help to remind me of that? How can I integrate that reminder into my daily life and spiritual practice?

Crafting a Cloth Totem

At the time I made my cloth totem, the only way to transfer the image onto fabric was by making a color photocopy of the image and ironing it onto unbleached muslin or similar fabric. With the years, happily, advances have made that literally involve only the click of a button!

Nowadays you can buy fabric-transfer paper at any craft store; they even have paper that will allow you to transfer a light image onto dark cloth. All you need to do is load your image onto your computer, adjust it to your needs using a photo program like Paint or Photoshop, print it, cut it out, peel off the backing and iron it onto your fabric! Things to remember: Angled shapes are more prone to peeling away from the fabric once ironed, so you might want to cut your image into more rounded shapes; and do note that anything that is white on your image, once transferred onto fabric, will be the color of that fabric. Be sure to follow the instructions that are printed on the box or included with the fabric-transfer paper, as those vary according to the brand you use.

You can fashion your totem's body in any way you like—it can be a doll, with limbs, or the cloth face can serve as the focus, with an oblong or other general shape as its "body." Embellishing it adds the final touch—you can find ribbon already imprinted with images or words that serve to underscore your reasons for choosing this person as a cloth totem; or you can add buttons, charms, and "clothing" that serves the same purpose.

"Someday, after mastering the winds, the waves, the tides and gravity, we shall harness for God the energies of love, and then, for a second time in the history of the world, man will have discovered fire."

—PIERRE TEILHARD DE CHARDIN

ANYTIME VALENTINES

Artist, mom, and volunteer Susan Hammack believes love should be expressed all the time, not just on Valentine's Day—though she first started her practice of making her "Anytime Valentines" on that holiday. Using small accordion-folded cards made of scraps of kraft paper cardstock, Susan collaged them with inspiring pictures and words, and attached charms. On each one, she handwrote the phrase "Dear beautiful friend," and then stated one small thing she truly appreciated about each person, such as "You inspire me" or "Thank you for supporting me."

Susan explains the impetus for her Anytime Valentines:

> I think that, as children, it is very natural to create with the intention of giving your drawing or handful of flowers to someone you love as an expression of your affection. As I grew and developed into various phases of my life, the form of that expression changed, but the heart of it was still very much the same.
>
> In grade school, hand-making paper valentines every year was a continuous reminder to me that I could employ my creativity in a way that helped others to feel loved and know that I valued them. I remember taking particular care in fourth grade as I hand-lettered valentines to my classmates, each inscribed with an outstanding quality I had noticed about them. I had fun watching their responses, which ranged from pleasure to embarrassment to surprise.
>
> As I grew into my teen years, I became famous for hand-illustrated letters

that were often in a novel format. A few of my favorites were a spiral chalk note written on the street that led to a mailbox filled with chocolate truffles; and a hallway wall at my high school covered in birthday wishes, caricatures, and random musings supplemented by a stack of fliers passed out to students to remind them of said birthday. As a young adult, I had a phase where I made novelty cakes for birthdays, holidays, and when loved ones were going into surgery. The most memorable were a smiling pig face, a mummy, and a uterus with a set of connected ovaries. Love takes so many forms!

Susan's efforts have reached around the world, when she saw the same concept behind her Valentines being used as "Truth Cards":

I recently spent two weeks in Nepal, studying expressive art therapy with trafficking survivors and conducting workshops with young girls in a safe house. We were encouraged to bring heartfelt gifts from home to share with the locals we came into contact with. I had brought with me a bag of "Truth Cards"—small, mixed-media creations the size of a playing card with positive and encouraging sentiments on them. They were made by women from all over the world and had been given to me so that I could spread the truths that we all are worthy and loved and that all things work together for good. They were so simple . . . a blob of paint here, a swatch of patterned paper there, a stamp of a bird, a drawing of a heart and a few kind words. The girls in the safe house were fighting over "the prettiest ones" and wanted them translated. They ran to their rooms to add them to their tiny stash of treasures, little things that reminded them that there is beauty in life. The women who trained us, survivors themselves, cradled them in their hands like lifelines. I'm sure they didn't cost much to make or even take that long, but the love they held travelled halfway across the world and moved hearts.

[For more information, and for instructions and a template for making Truth Cards, see bravegirlsclub.com/truth-card-exchange.]

When you hear stories like this, about how receiving an expression of acknowledgment can profoundly touch a life, it underscores the awareness that crafting as an expression of love is never frivolous and is not something we should postpone until conditions are "right." After all, as W. Somerset Maugham wrote, "Life isn't long enough for love and art."

Inner Inquiries for Journaling and Reflection

* ✳ How do I feel about making something for someone, rather than buying it?

* ✳ If I could give a "Truth Card" to someone, who would it be and what would it say?

Crafting a Practice

I have been crafting as long as I can remember. My first memory of losing myself in a creative act was when I was five years old. Everything else fell away as I brought egg carton ladybugs to life.

"In sixth grade, I read the book *Drawing on the Right Side of the Brain* by Betty Edwards. (Thank you Ms. Cashmark!) This was the first time I was aware that I was making a shift in my consciousness while drawing. From there it was possible for me to notice other times I connected with a deeper part of myself and when I was in my normal state. With awareness came the opportunity to practice and expand my capacity. This applies well beyond the craft room—which is good, because I don't have one of those! Being in that liminal space is spiritual for me. As far as making it a practice, I am still working on that rhythm.

"Several years ago, I stumbled upon the practice of intuitive drawing. I had been working with a bodyworker after being injured in a car accident and found that as she worked with my body, many powerful emotions and stories about my life began to emerge. The bodyworker suggested I 'draw my energy.' I wasn't even really sure what that meant, but I was open to try and felt that it needed to come from a raw, intuitive place that couldn't be censored by my ego. I used a four-by-six sketchbook, permanent markers, and small box of chalk pastels. I simply drew whatever my hand seemed to want to draw. It turned out to be a powerful lesson in trusting my intuition and non-judgment. So, I guess that means the most powerful resource is your instincts—follow them!

"Before you begin, take the time to connect with the love you are wanting to express. Perform a small ritual that helps you to focus on the sacredness of what you are about to do. Something as simple as lighting a candle or saying a brief prayer can instantly shift your mindset. Then, think about who or what it is you love and why. Feel it in your body. If your heart warms or you find yourself smiling, you are ready." —Susan Hammack

"You have within you more love than you could ever understand."

—RUMI

39

MEMORIAL PRAYER MATS

Picture a square of soft fabric, big enough to cover your lap. It looks like a cushion cover without stuffing. Finished on both sides, it lies flat. There are no zippers or flaps to open and insert pillow filling. Instead, one surface holds six sets of two embroidery threads waiting to be tied around special scrolled prayers or remembrances or actual mementoes. It is a fabric prayer mat, and while prayer mats can be made to hold all kinds of hopes and dreams—each set of

embroidery threads holding a specific intention or desire—this prayer mat is a little different. This prayer mat was made by Silvia Grady, to honor her late dear friend Daisy. At the time this book was being written, Silvia commented that her Memorial Prayer Mat was still a work in progress: "Once done I will be letting her go again in a way that brings me sadness—yet in another way, it's the beginning of a new practice to honor her and spend prayer time with her in Spirit. For this I am grateful!"

Silvia has been crafting for decades. As a professional educator and volunteer children's church program leader, she has had opportunities to keep crafting in the company of children. Silvia remembers how it all began, and how her parents' example not only demonstrated a love of crafting, but also their love for their family:

As a child I loved making things, starting out with mud pies, scrap pieces of paper or fabric, string, sticks, feathers . . . things that were found or just hanging around. Both my parents were very creative in ways that were fascinating to me. My father worked with wood and random materials, oftentimes making toys or gifts for us. We volunteered him to make a piñata for our school one year. He had us help by constructing the frame with thin willow branches, metal wire, and string. He then cooked up a concoction of glue made of flour and other mystery ingredients. We dipped strips of newspaper in that thick gooey substance and started the process of layering and covering the piñata frame. The last step was to cover the piñata with colorful tissue paper; he showed us how to delicately curl the ends. With those final touches, the piñata ended up looking like a clown!

My mom would transform cotton string into beautiful tablecloths or bedspreads, crocheting every interwoven tiny stitch to create the intricate patterns that would adorn our home. Since it sometimes took her years to complete a single piece, they became more than just a tablecloth or bedspread—they became part of the family! Flour sacks would become pillowcases, quilts, or patches for a worn garment. I would sit with my mom and learn from her with my own piece of string and crochet hook or needles, thread, and fabrics. Her specialty craft is cooking recipes that have been handed down to her from my great-great-grandmother and beyond. When I became a mom, my mother-in-law gifted me with a sewing machine, and that was the beginning of my love of quilting as my craft of choice.

Silvia, who was born in Mexico, continues her remembrances of how crafting became so important to her, and such a symbol of love itself:

I believe it started with my parents and my childhood. Looking back, it was more than just crafting—it was connecting with my parents. It takes care and love to show another or share with another the love of creating and expression through whatever form of medium is used. I began to see a connection with my ancestors through the teachings of my parents, and through their stories of how our grandparents would make their own candles, clothing, and hats, build their own homes, music, and food, and on and on. They learned a craft from their parents, who learned from their parents. I feel a connection to my ancestors when I am crafting, a love that comes from my connectedness with Spirit.

I especially began to feel my art/craft as a way of expressing love when I got involved in the early nineties with the Names Project AIDS Memorial Quilt in San Francisco. I was invited to help work on a quilt that was to be raffled off as a fundraiser for the project. I was overwhelmed by the beauty of the pieces being created by the loved ones of those who had died from AIDS. There are no words to express what each piece, each stitch, and each unique object, placed so lovingly on the panel, told of that particular person who was being honored. The love that shone through the smiles, laughter, and tears of the many people who were coming together to create and memorialize their loved ones was overwhelming. Pure love—this is what was being expressed through us . . . the love and compassion we have for another, whether they have transitioned or not.

Silvia notes that her Memorial Prayer Mat has ties to the memorial quilts she made during this time and continues to make:

My memorial quilts include fabrics from clothing, shirts, dresses, ties, scarfs, photo transfers onto cloth, anything the loved one wants included in the quilt. Twenty years later, my mom finds comfort in wrapping herself in the memorial quilt I made for her out of my dad's old work shirts and dress shirts.

I began making Memorial Prayer Mats recently, after becoming a lay prayer chaplain for my church and after the loss of a dear friend. I find prayer as a spiritual practice to be my connection to Spirit. When I combine this practice with my craft, I can sit in prayer with my Memorial Prayer Mat and feel even more connected to Spirit and to my loved ones who have passed. I feel very blessed for this connection.

Life itself is so transitory. What a lovely way to honor a loved one who has passed, by creating something that you can hold in prayer, possibly made of material that actually came from the clothing the person wore, or embellished with words or charms

> "Love is the great miracle cure. Loving ourselves works miracles in our lives."
>
> –LOUISE L. HAY

that signify who the person was. With a Memorial Prayer Mat—something tangible you can see and feel—those who have touched our lives will surely stay in our hearts forever.

Inner Inquiries for Journaling and Reflection

* How have I privately memorialized my beloveds—family, friends, pets—who have passed?

* Whose memory do I feel called to honor at this time in my life? What practice could I enfold into my life that would help me to do that?

"Do not waste time bothering whether you 'love' your neighbor; act as if you did. As soon as we do this, we find one of the great secrets. When you are behaving as if you loved someone, you will presently come to love him."

–C. S. LEWIS

Making a Memorial Prayer Mat

If sewing or quilting is a craft that you have already mastered, then your options can include using pieces of fabric from your loved one's clothing, as Silvia did when she used pieces from her father's work and dress shirts, to make a patchwork for your mat. If you don't quilt or sew, you can still make a Memorial Prayer Mat by finding or buying a cushion cover and adding personalized flourishes to that.

If you want to include the embroidery-thread sets that can hold a rolled-up prayer, written memory, or poem, simply add them from the inside of your cushion cover, leaving the knot where it can't be seen. You can also add charms or other embellishments to your Prayer Mat, or use fabric markers to write sentiments or the person's name.

45

CRAFTING LOVE:
FAMILY

CRAFTING LOVE:
FAMILY

In family life, love is the oil that eases friction, the cement that binds closer together,
and the music that brings harmony.
—EVA BURROWS

AH, FAMILIES . . . IN NO OTHER RELATIONSHIP IS THERE SO
much potential for the heights of joy and the depths of estrangement, perhaps simply
because there are more people involved with whom to experience this spectrum of
feeling. Whether we were born into one, adopted into one, or created one, the sense of
belongingness that being a part of a family both promises and offers is a very important
part of the human experience.

As anyone who has ever been part of a family knows—and that's most, if not all, of
us—it can be pretty easy to take those in our family for granted. Since they're part of
our day-to-day world, whether now or earlier in our lives, they're just supposed to "get"

that we love them, right? Well . . . since we all have probably fallen down on the job of expressing our love for our family members, the answer is "no." It's always appropriate and appreciated when we let those with whom we share our lives know that we do.

Though we may have cherished family traditions that we've created—some of which may even center around expressing love to a particular family member—it can only add to our relationships to increase the number of times we demonstrate it. So, toward that end, this section offers five ideas for honoring and celebrating our family members, both distant and near, long-ago and present-day. We should never lose sight of how lucky we are to have a family, even (or especially) on those days when we're not feelin' it. As one anonymous philosopher reminds us, "Having somewhere to go is home. Having someone to love is family. Having both is a blessing."

"The things that matter most in our lives are not fantastic or grand. They are moments when we touch one another, when we are there in the most attentive or caring way. This simple and profound intimacy is the love that we all long for."

–JACK KORNFIELD

ANCESTORS WATCH

For many cultures, respecting their elders, their ancestors, is so deeply embedded that it's not even consciously thought about—it is just something that you do. Traditionally, Korean and Chinese children take care of their elders as they age; Native American elders are respected and looked to for their life learnings; Greek elders are identified with wisdom and closeness to God. We in America don't always share that veneration—in fact, it sometimes seems as though it's the exception in our culture, rather than the rule.

One of my mentors, the late Angeles Arrien, frequently talked about the importance of honoring our ancestors. She often stated that, according to cross-cultural teachings, they are always around us: "Our male ancestors—the great-grandfathers, our grandfathers, our fathers, our uncles, our brothers—stand behind us on the right side, and our female ancestors—the great-grandmother, the grandmother, the mother, the sister, the aunt—stand behind us on the left side. And they say, 'Oh, maybe *this* one will be the one who will bring forward the good, true, and beautiful from all the past generations and the generations to come. Maybe *this* one will be the one who will bring the end to all the harmful family patterns, maybe *this* one will be the one."

Most importantly, Angeles taught that no matter how complicated our relationships might have been with our ancestors while they were alive, once they are in spirit form, they are there to love, watch over, and help us. And what better way to be reminded of our ancestors than to keep their image in front of us? A locket has been one way to do that, but a locket's treasures are kept hidden inside. Why not create a reminder that our ancestors watch over us by making an Ancestors Watch?

> "Love, love, love, that is the soul of genius."
>
> —WOLFGANG AMADEUS MOZART

Using the same idea behind a traditional locket, one can craft an expression of their love for an admired ancestor, or their awareness of the continuing presence of an ancestor in their life, by using an old watch (one of theirs, one of yours, something found at a flea market or yard sale) that cannot be repaired. Simply swap the clockworks for a reduced-size photograph of your ancestor, using the watch's lens as the front of the "frame."

Mahatma Gandhi said that "where there is love, there is life"—and by lovingly creating a way in which your ancestors can be remembered, truly they do live on.

Inner Inquiries for Journaling and Reflection

* Who among my ancestors—ancestors both of blood and of spirit— inspires me the most? Why?

* What qualities do I hope to pass on to future generations? Am I living those qualities on a daily basis? What can I do to help myself remember the legacy I hope to pass on?

ONE-A-DAY PILLBOX PRESENTS

For some odd reason, I seem to be drawn to plastic pillboxes—those miniature, lidded organizers you can find in drugstores or the "dollar bins" at various stores. Found in different transparent, translucent, or solid plastic of many colors, these little boxes have seven (or more) compartments and are usually marked with numbers or the days of the week, to denote their use as containers for medications taken daily. Oh, but they're useful for much more than that—they're wonderful containers for taking pierced earrings on a trip, placing small pendants with thin chains that can tangle, and, as it turns out, for crafting an expression of love to your family members.

I have compartmented pill boxes in a number of shapes—the rectangular is the most usual, but you can also find them in squares and circles, and sometimes with an attractive cloth cover that zips around the container. Those are the ones that are particularly nice

for One-a-Day Pillbox presents, a gift that's personal and perfect for both your children and parents alike.

Use each compartment for a tiny token of your love—a small note, a piece of candy, a pocket charm, or all three. The compartments are separate and usually labeled with one through seven for a week (more for larger containers), weekday names or abbreviations, and even times of day (morning, noon, evening) to signify when the medication is to be taken. This means the pleasure of your gift can be prolonged as the recipient opens up one (or more) compartments per day.

Let's stick with a simple seven-day pillbox. How can this be used? What about giving one to your spouse, to open at lunchtime, as he or she navigates the first week of a new job? Or to your child, as he or she experiences the first week of middle school or summer camp? Or to your parent making the transition from home ownership to assisted living? One-a-Day Pillbox Presents can be given as a "thinking of you" gift, when you have to leave for a business trip or as a little touchstone when your family member is spending overnights in a hospital.

Because the format is ready-made, they're easy to embellish—just personalize, fill, and present to your loved one. For most people, one expression of love a day is just what the doctor ordered!

Inner Inquiries for Journaling and Reflection

    ✳   Who in my family–current or family of origin–have I not been fully present to recently? Who's in need of a love "prescription"?

    ✳   Who in my family is undergoing some kind of transition right now? What might that person most need to hear to help that transition be smooth and successful?

FAMILY APPRECIATION JARS

With the exception of one's birthday, we have few opportunities to make someone feel like Queen—or King—of the Day. Yes, there's Valentine's Day, but that holiday is usually relegated to our romantic partners. (Interestingly, that is not true around the world. In countries ranging from Estonia to Guatemala, Finland to South Korea, friends and family members are also celebrated on this day.) But there are times in every person's life when it's not enough to know that you are loved and appreciated by your family members—it's important to know *why*. With the busyness of everyday life, we don't usually take the time to articulate the many reasons why someone close to you is so precious, but taking the time to do so is always worth the effort.

That effort can be eased somewhat by creating a container for every member of the household you live with—a Family Appreciation Jar. If you can find the right number, you can also use kitchen canisters for this purpose—perhaps decreasing in size according to the age of the family member. By having an individualized Appreciation Jar in place, family members can write notes throughout the year to acknowledge each other, to let each other know when they appreciated something about that person, saw something special in him or her, or just plain felt a burst of affection.

It doesn't take too much imagination to realize how powerful this practice can be. After all, wouldn't *you* like to dip into a jar and find notes that express appreciation of your qualities and skills? As adults, we can make that happen by setting up this system of acknowledgment for our families.

Depending on the material of what you're using, the Family Appreciation Jars or canisters could be decorated with permanent-ink pens and paints. Or if they're transparent—made of glass or clear plastic—family members could make their own collage on a piece of rectangular paper that's cut to size, placed, and affixed to the inside of the jar, image-side out. If your family members don't consider themselves crafty types, you can make one for each person. The most important thing is to ensure that each family member has a designated container into which expressions of love and appreciation can be placed.

Ideas for what to comment on range from the very specific to more general categories. Possibilities for writing a note of appreciation include acknowledgment of hard work or sustained effort on a task, congratulations for an achievement or goal met, celebration of a particular quality or behavior, reassurance for one going through a period of uncertainty, and even just a "I love you because of the funny and cute way you talk to the cats" is good fodder for your jar!

How to use the jar can become your own family tradition. You might want to take turns reading notes once a week, on a Family Game Night or Family Movie Night, once a month, on the person's birthday, or once a year on a significant day such as Thanksgiving or New Year's Eve. What's crucial is simply getting into the habit of doing it, for there's nothing like seeing something in writing to help us take those words to heart. Through this practice, we fulfill the words of novelist Joseph Conrad, who said, "My task, which I am trying to achieve is, by the power of the written word, to make you hear, to make you feel—it is, before all, to make you see." *We* see the all the beauty and grace in our family members—this way, they can see it too.

Inner Inquiries for Journaling and Reflection

* What is the kindest thing a family member has ever said about me? Was it a written appreciation, or a spoken one? What made that sentiment feel so important to me?

* Do I have a system in my family for receiving words of acknowledgment? How might dynamics in my family change if we did have one?

"Let your heart crumble into an infinite amount of tiny, precious seeds. Then plant love everywhere you go."

—ANITA KRIZZAN

CONVERSATION-STARTER TABLECLOTH

The writer Anne Morrow Lindbergh once said, "Good communication is as stimulating as black coffee and just as hard to sleep after." While we may not want to have family conversations that make it hard to sleep—especially if we have little ones!—the point is well taken: There are few things as inspiring and potentially life-changing as a great conversation.

In families that are juggling different schedules and phases of life, it can be difficult to find the time to have those kinds of deep, enriching talks. But statistics consistently show how important it is to share meals with your kids, to talk to them about the big questions of life as well as the little details. Sadly, most of us don't do this—the number of meals most American families eat together has plummeted, and when we do eat together, no less than one-third of us report having the television on!

In addition to the obvious emotional drawbacks of this behavior in nurturing our relationships and keeping them fresh, it's also affecting us in other ways. According to one report, a teen's chance of smoking, drinking, and using drugs is drastically lowered when family dinners are shared at least five times a week. Teens who who have fewer than three family dinners a week are 3.5 times more likely to have abused prescription drugs, three times more likely to have used marijuana, more than 2.5 times more likely to have smoked cigarettes, and 1.5 times more likely to have tried alcohol.

Have I made the case for family dinners? As the mother of a preteen at the time I write this book, learning such statistics certainly solidified my resolve to consistently have family meals. And if, like me, you have a child or children for whom "Nothing" is a complete sentence—as in, "What happened in school today?" "Nothing."—you might be interested in making a Conversation-Starter Tablecloth.

While there are many products on the market that pose questions for conversation, many of them in card form, it can be clunky to pull out a box of cards with questions on them while one is actually trying to eat. With the questions already printed or embroidered on the very tablecloth your plates are on, creating conversations becomes a lot easier.

For many, this exercise harkens back to Thanksgiving dinner games. In fact, if you're looking for ideas for questions to put on your tablecloth, you will find many suggestions in articles about conversation rituals at holiday time. Examples

> "We come to love not by finding a perfect person, but by learning to see an imperfect person perfectly."
> –SAM KEEN

are: "What would you do if you won a million dollars?" (Or, adjusting for inflation, five million dollars.) "What was your most embarrassing moment?" "What is your earliest childhood memory?"

You'll want to pick questions that family members of all ages can answer—and, if you anticipate using the tablecloth regularly, you may want to create more than one Conversation-Starter Tablecloth. This may be your own project, and presented to the family with your selection of questions already on it, or you may want to enroll your family members in this activity by asking them for their suggestions of questions to include.

Like other crafts in this book, your approach to this can be as simple or involved as you wish. You can make your own tablecloth, use one you already have, or purchase new. Embroider the questions on it, or you can simply use fabric markers to "write" your questions on the tablecloth you'll be using—or both! Whichever way you approach your Conversation-Starter Tablecloth, one thing is assured: an opportunity to engage your family in a conversation over a meal. As Miriam Weinstein—the author of *The Surprising Power of Family Meals*—put it, "Sitting down to a meal together draws a line around us. It encloses us and strengthens the bonds that connect us with other members of our self-defined clan, shutting out the rest of the world." Any questions?

Inner Inquiries for Journaling and Reflection

* What are my memories of family meals? What was conversation like when I was growing up? As a child, was I encouraged to converse or not?

* What would I most like to know about my family members—what are the conversations I would most like to have with them? What are some gentle questions that would invite a response about those areas of their lives?

FAMILY TREES

Though mother-in-law jokes abound, I sure hit the jackpot with my mother-in-law, Donna Shannon. I will always be so grateful to her for the wonderful things she said and did as a grandmother to my daughter at a time when my own mother was starting a rapid descent into dementia. Every conceivable holiday was celebrated with a special card and little "care package" of thematic gifts—from Beanie Baby jack-o'-lanterns to Valentine's Day hair clips. My daughter was always remembered with thoughtful expressions of love. Sadly, my mother-in-law passed away after struggling with dementia herself, but her thoughtful acts live on in our memories . . . and, as it so happens, in the side yard of the family farm.

Ever one to create special rituals, Donna planted a living tree for each of her grandchildren. My daughter is the youngest, so her cousins' trees are larger and more established than hers is. But every time we visit the farm where her father grew up and her grandfather still lives, my daughter Chloe goes straight to her tree—it is a living, and still evolving, symbol of the joy her grandparents felt when Chloe became part of the Shannon family.

There are more traditional ways to craft a family tree—a photo collage or sampler comes immediately to mind—but literally planting "family trees" is a powerful way to express love. It both honors the person and illustrates hope for the future—and makes for great photographs, as your child stands next to his or her tree, growing ever taller along with it.

If you're an apartment dweller and don't have the land to plant a tree, there are variations on this theme. One could choose an indoor tree (there are actually indoor fruit trees!), a bonsai tree, or even an herb garden to celebrate the new life and new branches of your family tree. Whatever environment you're working with, using the art of gardening in the service of celebrating a family member is a meaningful expression—as the Sufi poet Rumi wrote, "With life as short as a half-taken breath, don't plant anything but love."

Inner Inquiries for Journaling and Reflection

* Were there any special traditions celebrated when I became part of the family, either by birth or by marriage? (For instance, my mother-in-law, Donna, bought me my choice of a large Waterford-crystal vase to use for the roses her son would be getting me—and he does!)

* What rituals or traditions does my family have now for celebrating new additions to the family tree? What could I craft that would be meaningful not only to the recipient, but also to every member of the family?

What Trees Symbolize

If you like this idea of planting or growing a live tree to celebrate someone joining the family, there are folkloric associations with certain types of trees. Below is a list—most of these are from the Celtic tradition—that may inform and inspire your choice:

Ash: seen as the guardian of children, and symbolizes growth, higher awareness, and sensitivity.

Apple: considered a symbol of creativity, love, and virtue; also associated with being healthy and immortality.

Birch: symbolizes adaptability, renewal, and stability; also has an association with cleansing the past.

Elm: associated with intuition and strength of will.

Fir: represents fortitude, hope, longevity, and resilience.

Maple: symbolizes balance, practicality, and promise.

Oak: this "king of trees" symbolizes courage, life, strength, and wisdom.

Willow: symbolizes adaptability, flexibility, dreams, and imagination.

CRAFTING LOVE:
NATURE—PLACES AND ANIMALS

Chapter 4:

CRAFTING LOVE:
NATURE — PLACES AND ANIMALS

> "If you are not radiant with joy and friendliness, if you are not filled to
> overflowing with love and goodwill for all beings and all creatures and all
> creation, one thing is certain: you do not know God!"
> —PEACE PILGRIM

THOUGH FREQUENT USERS OF THE WORD "LOVE" TO DESCRIBE
their feelings for everything ranging from ice cream to Ice-T can be criticized for a lack
of specificity and discernment in their word choice, the fact is that we as humans do love
many things. Yes, of course, the quality of our love differs according to the object of it.
We have a much deeper quality of love for our child, say, than we do for our favorite TV
show, but we do find our hearts opening at all kinds of "awe-some" things in this world.
Things we love include favorite places as well as other living beings with whom we share
this wide world . . . we love butterflies or blue jays and especially we love our pets, those
animals, birds and reptiles we've chosen to be our companions in life.

In this section, you'll read about ways to express that love whose object is Nature—both in the grandest scale (a golden sunset over the Grand Canyon, say) and in the tiniest (an apple-green baby caterpillar inching its way along a leaf). It is a transcendent love, a love that takes us out of ourselves and connects us to the Universe itself. We would do well to heed the words of Fyodor Dostoevsky, who wrote: "Love all the earth, every ray of God's light, every grain of sand or blade of grass, every living thing. If you love the earth enough, you will know the divine mystery."

"Love is a powerful healing energy. Our world can benefit from more loving prayers for improved health. Take some time right now to share some loving words from someone you know who could benefit from some extra kindness. Or offer love in silent meditation—either to a specific person or in a general way to all the beings in this world who are presently suffering in some way."

—KAREN SALMANSOHN

PORTABLE PLACE SHRINES

Every other summer, my husband, daughter, and I travel to the other side of the country to spend a week at a place that has come to feel like a second home, a seasonal retreat in which we hope to someday live for more than the biannual week. That place is Chautauqua Institution in New York, a uniquely American summer "camp" for all ages.

Founded in 1874, this nonprofit organization started as a teaching camp for Sunday school teachers. In the years since, it has grown into a respected adult-education center and summer resort that has hosted religious, political, and intellectual luminaries from around the world. Featuring arts, education, and religious programs as well as world-class performances and lectures, Chautauqua also offers short special-studies courses taught by selected visitors. I have had the good fortune for several years to teach short classes there during my stay. One summer, at one of the annual craft fairs Chautauqua hosts, I purchased something that enchanted me then and continues to inspire me now. A small, circular tin with a clear-glass lid, only two inches in diameter, is a veritable "time capsule" of some of the delights that Chautauqua holds. There are little beads—ranging from a hematite heart to a glazed clay oval—representing crafts classes (like some of the ones I've taught!) you can take during your time there; a miniature pencil, to represent writing notes during the lectures offered each morning and afternoon; bits of lace, a doll-sized embroidered pillow, and a tiny teacup to represent the joys of the ubiquitous outdoor porches; a blue plastic butterfly and black plastic bat, to represent some of the winged creatures found in Chautauqua skies; a silk rose the size of a fingernail, to reference the gorgeous summer blooms; the tiniest sheet of music, to denote the many concerts given on the grounds; a minuscule framed picture of the Chautauqua bell tower accompanied by a small brass bell.

Sadly, I have no record of who it is who made this wonderful little shrine, but it delights me every time I look at it. I am reminded of the place I love. None of the many elements in this skillful composition of tiny items measures more than an inch-and-a-half. It is a way to carry Chautauqua with me, though the actual place is located 3,000 miles from where I live.

If you love the idea of having a portable shrine representing a place close to your heart (if not your actual body), they are easy to create. Craft stores carry an abundance of little containers you could use for your shrine, such as the tin circle with see-through lid I described, or transparent colored or clear plastic boxes. Be on the lookout, too, for breath-mint containers. Not only can they be altered (Altoid tins are especially great for portable shrines), but often you can find higher-priced black plastic mint boxes featuring a work of art, deity, or scenic landscape on the cover. (I found one depicting Chautauqua's bell tower, and purchased it thinking I'd transfer the contents of the little shrine

> "Only love can be divided endlessly and still not diminish."
> —ANNE MORROW LINDBERGH

I bought to it, but I like peeking through the glass lid at all the contents too much to make the trade.)

Once you've selected your "shrine," you can decorate the outside any way you want—but the true joy is found in picking the tiny treasures to place inside. In that action, we can learn so much about ourselves; we can literally see, in the words of Rumi, that "whatever you love, you are."

Inner Inquiries for Journaling and Reflection

* What places do I love? Which ones do I feel I carry in my heart? Can I articulate why they mean so much to me? What do I feel there?

* What little tokens best symbolize what I love about those places—and why?

HEARTS IN NATURE

It still has a place of honor in my front foyer—a sculpture, just over twenty-eight inches high, composed from a heart-shaped piece of driftwood. A metal rod stuck into a driftwood base holds the heart aloft—smooth to the touch, oiled to a dark lacquer-like sheen, it is a symbol and celebration of my wedding, made for me by a beloved former boss who is no longer alive.

That right there is a good reason to craft something for another—when you are separated, whether by distance, life circumstances, or death, your handmade gift contains your energetic imprint; all I have to do is look at or touch this

> "The flute of the Infinite is played without ceasing, and its sound is Love."
>
> —KABIR

sculpture to be reminded of Wink Franklin, the wonderful man who made it. Other wedding gifts I received still spark an affectionate memory of who gave it to us—the ceramic candy dish, the silver bottle opener, the glass flower vase—but this driftwood sculpture stands apart. I know its maker's hands carefully sanded or oiled the textures I touch. I assume I was at least briefly thought of during the making of the piece and that somehow this sculpture contains that thought too. There is something about the material that feels special to me—it comes from nature, which created an organic piece that looks like the symbol for a heart from one side, or like two strong arms outstretched toward a sky of possibility on the other.

When we look at nature we are invited to put our own interpretation onto what we're seeing—to name what that amorphous cloud looks like, or how this glorious sunrise makes us feel. When the answer is obvious—it looks like a heart—then we become delighted at the jokester (or the Trickster) behind the wonderful surprise of finding a heart in a piece of driftwood. Indeed, heart shapes found in nature are so well loved that there are entire Pinterest boards and blogs devoted to them, photographic collections that show the vast array of natural heart shapes discovered: heart-shaped islands, leaves, pebbles; heart-shaped clouds, animal spots, flora. We are delighted because we feel love is all around us, that all we have to do is gaze carefully and we will find love everywhere we look.

Though not all of us have the technical proficiency to or interest in sanding down driftwood, we can use other heart-shaped natural finds to make a gift that both demonstrates love for the gift recipient and denotes our love of nature. As we peruse natural settings for heart-shaped finds, we are experiencing nature in a different way; we are expecting it to delight us when we search for symbols of love.

Once you've found heart-shaped shells, rocks, leaves, or pieces of wood, there are all kinds of creative possibilities. What to do with your heart-shaped finds runs the gamut from stand-alone sculpture, such as the one I just described; making wind chimes; using your finds to adorn a mirror or photo frame; gluing them atop a painted box; making jewelry out of smaller pieces; or simply displaying them in a bowl, where they are able to be picked up and admired.

If you really find yourself enthralled by the hunt for hearts, you can take a cue from others who have started blogs detailing where they've found or seen the hearts; start a Pinterest board devoted to heart shapes (I have one myself: pinterest.com/revmaggie/

hearts.) You might open an Etsy shop devoted to your heart art. There are communities you can join, such as the "Hearts in Nature" on Facebook, set up expressly for people who love hearts.

It's said the Divine speaks to us in symbols, and that philosophy is hard to argue with when we start to spy symbols of love all around us in nature. Kind of makes you feel that the Universe—well, to use the words from Paul Simon's song—that the Universe loves us like a rock!

Inner Inquiries for Journaling and Reflection

     ✳   Have I ever come across heart shapes in nature before? If so, what was the feeling I experienced—joy, awe, amusement, amazement?

     ✳   Do I see recurring heart shapes in nature as a symbol of a benevolent Universe? How can I use these little symbols as a reminder that I am loved?

ANIMAL MEDICINE BAGS

Though I am a lifelong animal lover, I was well into my thirties before I started thinking about animals as totems—representations of a certain kind of energy or quality I might want to bring into the world. I knew there were particular mammals, reptiles, insects, and birds I was drawn to more than others. I have always loved the iridescence of dragonflies, for example, and been captivated the mystery of owls. But I didn't know how deep and rich the folklore is behind all creatures until I took a personal-growth class shortly after moving to San Francisco in the mid-nineties.

On the first evening of this class, the teacher presented us with a deck of cards unlike any I had seen before. She explained they were "Animal Medicine Cards" and that we would be picking one to guide us through the rest of the class and its in-depth explorations. I remember looking at the identical backs of the cards, wondering which creature would reveal itself to me as my guide . . . and the feeling of immediate disappointment I felt when I drew a bat. *Bat?* Other women in the class got *cute* animals, *fun* animals like Otter. Why did I have to choose Bat?! Such was the tenor of my unenlightened (and uninitiated) inner dialogue after drawing this unwanted card.

But Bat started working its magic on me, and now I feel very fond of that totem. No, it's not a "cute" animal, or a "fun" animal, but it's an extremely potent animal symbolically. Bat, I learned, is a powerful totem with deep significance: it signals rebirth, transformation, spiritual initiation.

It can be extremely meaningful to work with an animal totem; they can serve as a lens through which to explore aspects of your life and experience. Knowing the folk-loric symbolism behind various birds, insects, mammals, and reptiles helps one to better appreciate the fullness of Nature's arc. (See sidebar on page 78.)

One of the assignments for the class was to create a "medicine bag" that incorporated our animal totem in some way. I was not at all sure where I was going to find an image of a bat, since we were on the other end of the seasonal cycle from Halloween and I hadn't noticed a profusion of bat items in most retail establishments. But by chance—or was it Divine design?—I did find one in a gallery specializing in Native American art and hand-crafts: a small, two-inch high baby bat carved out of deer antler. I still have that bat fetish (such carvings are usually done by the Zuni tribe, and are called "fetishes"), and while I no longer carry it in a pouch around my neck, it remains a powerful symbol for me.

A medicine bag comes from some Native American tribal traditions. It is a small bag, usually no more than two to four inches high, with a long drawstring that can be placed around your neck, keeping your "medicine"—the sacred and symbolic contents of the pouch—close to your heart. I no longer remember what it was that I placed in my bat medicine bag, other than the fetish itself, but I imagine I included ingredients I have used in subsequent medicine bags—a small stone or two, an affirmation or prayer rolled up into a tiny scroll, leaves of tobacco, lavender buds, or another herb.

If you'd like to make an Animal Medicine Bag, you'll find basic instructions below. You can also find ready-made leather (and other material) pouches in craft stores and on

> "The way of peace is the way of love. Love is the greatest power on earth. It heals all things."
>
> —PEACE PILGRIM

Etsy, some adorned with the image, feathers, or fur of the creature itself. Whether you decide to craft your own medicine bag or to embellish an existing one, immersing yourself in the qualities of your chosen totem will enhance your love for that species—as well as enhance the qualities of that being that you have set before you to increase or emulate. Increasing our appreciation for the other beings we share the planet with is always a worthy impulse. It reminds me of the poignant words of astronomer Carl Sagan: "For small creatures such as we the vastness is bearable only through love."

Inner Inquiries for Journaling and Reflection

* What animals have I always been drawn to? (Try to think of one for each animal class: mammal, bird, fish, reptile, insect, and amphibian—raccoon, swan, shark, lizard, dragonfly, and frog, for example.)

* What unusual animal sighting have I had recently? Has any creature crossed my path in an unusual or unexpected way? What might that creature have to teach me about what's going on in my life?

Animal Totem Characteristics

Once you have discovered what animal feels most resonant with you, it can be richly rewarding to discover what characteristics are assigned to that creature through folklore, indigenous teachings, and other sources. One of my favorite reference books is *Animal-Speak: The Spiritual & Magical Powers of Creatures Great & Small* by the late Ted Andrews. Set up as a dictionary of sorts, it provides useful (and fascinating) information about a wide selection of species. Here are some common animal, insect, and bird totems and brief associations to get you started:

Ant: Little Ant is industrious, and thus can show us how to build our dreams, architect our future, by working with others.

Bat: As I found out, Bat signifies transitions into a new identity—facing the darkness in order to turn to the light, rebirth.

Cat: Anyone who's ever been near a cat will not be surprised to learn Cat represents independence and self-sufficiency.

Bear: Perhaps not surprisingly, Bear signifies leadership qualities, strength, and courage.

Dragonfly: Dragonfly brings light and color into your life—the magic of transformation.

Eagle: Eagle is a powerful totem that calls people to new perceptions, new zeniths.

Frog: Because of the way in which it grows—from tadpole to fully formed frog—Frog is a symbol of metamorphosis. (I have also always liked Frog for the acronym that its name spells out: Fully Rely on God.)

Horse: Freedom and power—personal drive—are what Horse represents.

Lizard: Lizard is frequently associated with dreams and regeneration.

Mouse: Like the ant, Mouse is industrious and organized—and this totem may be asking you to look at what is right before you.

Otter: Otter is a joyous totem, representing freedom and play.

Owl: As anyone who's ever seen a Harry Potter movie will tell you, Owl represents secret knowledge and the ability to see things that others might miss.

Snake: Because of the way it sheds its skin, Snake is a symbol of transformation and represents healing and wisdom.

Spider: Spiders (yes, an animal of the class arachnid!) represent creativity, and are an especially potent totem for writers—those who "weave with words."

Turtle: Turtle is an ancient totem, the symbol for Earth itself.

DIY: Making a Medicine Bag

To make a simple medicine bag, you will need a circle of leather or heavy fabric (approximately eight inches or less in diameter if you want to hang it around your neck), a leather punch or hole punch, leather cord or satin cord to use as the drawstrings, and beads and other embellishments, if desired.

Punch holes approximately an inch apart around the edge of your circle. Thread your cord down through one hole and up through the next, until your cord has gone through all the holes in the circle. When done, make sure the two ends of cord go up in the same direction. Punch one final hole if necessary to make sure the two ends can both be pulled from the outside of the bag. String small beads on each cord, if desired, then knot the two cord ends together tightly. Pulling on the cords should draw the material together, making a pouch you can place your animal totem inside.

NATURAL PATTERNS

For Holly Byram, the love of nature is a constant inspiration. It not only prompts her art, but soothes her soul. As Holly expresses it, "Nature is where I have often gone to be quiet and spiritually renewed. My love of nature and its infinite variety and beauty often ends up in my work—it speaks back to the exquisite natural design that surrounds us."

A quick look at some of the pieces Holly has created shows a diversity of artistic skills, but a certain constancy of focus. Working primarily with mosaic, paint, and chain maille, there are natural echoes—patterns that are repeated—throughout her work. For instance, a painting called "Day of the Iguana" realistically displays a lizard in full yellow-green splendor; a similar shade of yellow-green rings is used in a chain maille necklace dubbed "Poison Serpent." Perhaps because she combines different mediums in her work, we can note new relationships or similarities in patterns found in nature when we experience her art.

Holly has been expressing herself creatively for most of her life, but has only recently started to see her passion for creating has a spiritual component:

> I have been crafting and/or making art since I was very young. It has been one of the few constants in my life—no matter what transitions I have gone through, the drive to create has stayed with me. I have expressed my ideas through various media over the years, seeking the best "language" to reveal what was inside of me. It has only been in recent years that I really came to

view the creative process as a spiritual practice. Something in my soul drives me, and I cannot ignore the drive, though it may go dormant sometimes if I am dealing with a lot of life issues. I cannot not do it, and I see it as one of the most natural and authentic parts of my being. Sometimes I enjoy it, and sometimes it is nothing but struggle, but the work must nevertheless be done.

It was Nature itself that helped Holly to see that what she was doing was a way of expressing her love for it:

I think I realized art was a way of expressing love about ten years ago, when I began doing photography and painting things from nature. I adore the natural world and the vast diversity that lies therein; it is endlessly fascinating and beautiful to me. If I can capture something with a lens, or interpret a creature through any other art medium, I can connect with it, and get to know it in a deeper, more meaningful way. That connection is love. I express my love of the subject, and the world, through the creation of my art.

Making a mindfulness practice out of creatively observing, and then translating, nature as Holly does, not only helps us to see natural patterns but also to see—to even love—the object itself. To begin, notice if what you take photos of in nature—for instance, flowers—also have colors you've used in another art form, such as knitting or painting. Or look to see if the iridescence of a shell, for instance, prompts the use of iridescence in a mosaic. The question to ask is always: What are the patterns? Where are the similarities? It's important to look. As Georgia O'Keeffe once wrote, "Nobody sees a flower—really—it is so small it takes time—we haven't time—and to see takes time, like to have a friend takes time."

Inner Inquiries for Journaling and Reflection

* What in the natural world most inspires me—animals, flowers, rocks, trees? How can I stay plugged into those sources of inspiration?

* Are there ways in which an inspiration in one area of my life is echoed in another? Do I use similar colors, shapes, patterns in the different forms of creative expression that I practice?

"But love, I've come to understand, is more than three words mumbled before bedtime. Love is sustained by action, a pattern of devotion in the things we do for each other every day."
—NICHOLAS SPARKS

Crafting a Practice

For those who want to start a creative-expression practice, Holly has these words of wisdom:

> My practice has been a slow, quiet evolution. I have contemplated my work, and my philosophy regarding my work, drawing from so many things around me like a sponge. It would be difficult to pinpoint specific resources that have helped me along the way, as it has been such a gradual process for me. I have focused most recently on creating mosaic and jewelry; however, different ideas call for different media. I used to berate myself for not sticking to one particular mode of expression because I was told I would never achieve mastery. However, I learn something new from each medium, and I return to old ones with a fresh perspective.
>
> I would tell someone to trust the creative process and loosen their hold on strict expectation. I have ideas in my head of how I want pieces to be, but then when I get into the flow of things, I let them talk to me. The magic happens when I get off-course and

let go of my idea of what something must be, and it becomes a meditation in motion. With mosaic, specifically, it is a puzzle that I have to piece together. Each piece tells me where it wants to go, and the tesserae tell me how they want to flow. Mosaic serves also as a perfect metaphor for my life—finding out how I best connect to everything else.

SMUDGE PRAYER FEATHERS

There is something so magical about feathers, the often bright-colored plumage that distinguishes birds from other species. Feathers have adorned religious ceremonial costumes for millennia in cultures ranging from ancient Egyptian to Native American. And who hasn't stopped to pick up a feather that has crossed your path? This is often viewed as a message from a dear one who has departed the Earth plane. Other people believe in the slogan that "when feathers appear, angels are near!"

Perhaps because they are symbols of flight, feathers are evocative. Other things a feather might symbolize would vary according to its color (yellow is seen as signifying the need to be alert, cheerful, light-hearted, for example; red is associated with courage, passion and strength) and its source (for instance, a dove feather is associated with gentleness, kindness, and love; an eagle feather with courage, leadership and strength).

Of course, the meaning of a feather might be individual to you. Two decades ago, I attended a modern-day Mystery School, and while I can't remember the context (nor should I repeat it, even if I could), I do remember having a sense of the afterlife as being a huge collection of white lotus-like feather flowers, each opening up to enfold its special soul into its softness. This positive association with white feathers continued into another personal context when I was suddenly hospitalized and for days doctors were unable to find the exact cause of my symptoms. I remember someone telling me I was in their prayers, and I had the visual image of resting in that same white lotus feather flower. I felt like each prayer said for me lifted me higher onto this soft, comforting bed of white feathers. To this day I associate white feathers with prayers.

If you, too, have a special affinity with feathers, then you will enjoy creating a practice using feathers as a primary focus. There are many crafts out there that you can choose—one that comes immediately to mind is the Native American dream-catcher, a hoop whose interior is webbed with cord or yarn in order to "catch dreams"; these are often adorned with a scanty fringe of feathers attached at the bottom of the hanging. One can also fashion jewelry out of feathers, or adorn scarves with them, to be used in a ceremonial way or simply to enjoy the sight of feathers during the day-to-day. But one of the most pleasurable ways to work creatively with feathers is by painting them—and using them as a Smudge Prayer Feather.

For those who are new to the practice, "smudging" a space by burning an herb considered sacred—such as white sage or sweetgrass, or even lavender—and fanning the smoke is considered a way to cleanse the space as well as to purify the

> "When we can do nothing else, we can still love, without expecting any reward or change or gratitude."
> —PAOLO COEHLO

energy of a person or object. Using a Smudge Prayer Feather for fanning the smoke into every corner of a room, or all around the person or object, is considered part of the ritual.

For those who are hesitating at the word "smoke," incense can also be used for smudging. Although it's usually associated with Native American spirituality, a form of smudging is used in cultures around the world. Catholic churches and cathedrals often use frankincense in their rituals; incense is part of the Jewish Havdalah service to mark the end of Sabbath; in Buddhist temples, incense sticks are burned continuously.

Whether or not one believes smudging is actually clearing a place or person of negative or old energy, it is a helpful ritual for marking new beginnings—and thus making your own Smudge Prayer Feather can become a very meaningful act.

Feathers of all shapes and sizes can be found in craft stores, but if you have found a particular feather on your path, that might be a powerful one to use. You can use a single feather or a group of feathers, bound together at the bottom, called a calamus, with some kind of material serving as the handle. Since this is a Smudge *Prayer* Feather, you want to be mindful in your selection and creation of it as a spiritual tool.

My Smudge Prayer Feather is a single painted feather approximately eight inches long. It is the color of an indigo night sky and painted with stars and a crescent moon. I have had it for many years; it is part of my spiritual "toolkit," and feels like an old friend. I keep it in an abalone shell that also holds a bundle of sage and part of a sweetgrass braid, my favorite herbs for smudging.

Smudging is a ritual I perform anytime I want to mark a fresh start—at the beginning of the year, on my birthday, after a big project is completed. Using my longtime Smudge Prayer Feather, I am able to, as Dinah McCraik put it, "Keep what is worth keeping, and with a breath of kindness blow the rest away."

Inner Inquiries for Journaling and Reflection

✻ Have I ever found a feather while walking around, either in the city or in nature? What association did I make with that? Where is the feather now?

✻ Do I have any kind of ritual for creating new beginnings, or for cleansing my space of old (and possibly negative) energy? What smells, colors, prayers would help me to feel that I had spiritually purified my environment?

CRAFTING LOVE:
SELF-LOVE

Chapter 5:

CRAFTING LOVE: SELF-LOVE

"You can search throughout the entire universe for someone who is more deserving of your love and affection than you are yourself, and that person is not to be found anywhere. You yourself, as much as anybody in the entire universe, deserve your love and affection."

–OFTEN ATTRIBUTED TO BUDDHA, BUT ACTUAL AUTHOR UNKNOWN

IT ALL STARTS AND STOPS WITH SELF-LOVE. IF WE CAN'T LOVE ourselves, how can we really love another? The problem is, as the wag Anthony Powell put it, that "self-love seems so often unrequited."

Many times we feel that cultivating, and certainly expressing, love for oneself is somehow unseemly; that if we profess self-love we're being arrogant, or self-absorbed— and definitely not "spiritual." But as some contemporaries have noted, for many spiritual people, the concept of *not* loving yourself is foreign. The Dalai Lama expressed it clearly when he said: "If you don't love yourself, you cannot love others. You will not be able to love others."

All the creative activities in this section are ways of exploring our own gifts and treasures, the sparking inner geode crystals that lie beneath the bumpy and perhaps bland surfaces of our lives. We can be confident as we go down this path that we are not being selfish but instead are deepening our capacity to love. As musician and writer Jaymie Gerard reminds us, "Loving yourself is healing the world!"

"Love isn't a state of perfect caring. It is an active noun, like struggle. To love someone is to strive to accept that person exactly the way he or she is, right here and now."

—FRED ROGERS

SELF-LOVE BOX

Visually, it is an explosion of joy. Painted in vibrant poppy red and gold, it's collaged with statements like "I love me!" and "Dance!" and "Defy Gravity!" Further festooned with images of stars, hearts, roses and other flowers, plus a little yellow bird, it features a small paper manifesto with these big words: "She spoke in exclamations . . . now that she found her voice."

For author and life coach Susyn Reeve, it is a Self-Love Box—a reminder that her inner world is as colorful and vibrant as the outside of her box. For Susyn, crafting this expression of self-love has been an evolution of her creative focus, which has been prolific through the years. "I've been crafting since I was a child," Susyn says, "making lanyards, knitting and crocheting, pen-and-ink drawings. I have sold macramé jewelry, breadbaskets made of dough, knitted scarves and beaded pouches, and needlepoint pillows and purses. I've always loved making gifts for family and friends—infusing the gifts with love."

But she adds:

> Crafting as a conscious spiritual practice began in the late 1990s when I started making "charmed creations"—small pouches made with beautiful ribbons and beads that were worn around the neck. Friends, family, and strangers asked me to make them. I told them to tell me the experience, quality, or feeling they wanted the pouch to evoke, and I'd think about that as well as

enclose a beautiful piece of paper in the finished product with their intention for the 'charmed creation' written on it.

Each of her "charmed creations," Susyn explains, was far more than what it might seem, as evidenced in the wording she would include about them: "Each charmed creation art piece is made as a prayer honoring and celebrating the creative process . . . the marriage of beauty and function, skill and imagination. Each piece is an affirmation to inspire you to be a charmed creation in all that you are and all that you do." Since then, Susyn says, "I've considered all my crafting to be creating 'charmed creations'!"

Susyn's Self-Love Box came about in the following way:

I was visiting my dear friend Calla Crafts—of course, with a last name like that, we often do crafts together! We were wondering what to make as a special seventieth birthday gift for one of our friends. In a spurt of inspiration I thought we could decoupage a number of boxes with images that are a reflection of our friend. We were both excited. When I visited Calla a few weeks later, we were armed with decoupage supplies! As I began painting, and cutting, and pasting and decoupaging, I had another spurt of inspiration. Rather than calling my new coaching work "Designing Your Third Act," since I'd loved and was good at crafts I would call my work "Crafting Your Next Chapter." And this first box became my 3-D vision board. I decoupaged every side, inside, outside, bottom, top as a reflection of my wholehearted life vision. I keep it open these days as a reminder that it is my inside that informs my outer world. One of my favorite quotes on the lid is from a birthday card a special friend sent to me. This Self-Love Box is an artistic expression of who I am—a self-portrait.

For Susyn, crafting is a conduit to self-discovery, a way not only to discover hidden gifts but also to cement deeply held intentions. Explains Susyn:

> In recent years I've done crafting with groups as a way for the participants to create shawls that evoke the quality or qualities they want to evoke in their lives. These days, with my work focusing on "Crafting Your Third Act," each part of the program centers on a concept—such as completing the past, articulating your vision, et cetera—that is further expressed through a crafting project.
>
> Creating Self-Love Boxes is now an integral part of my work—inviting others to step "out of the box" and create or craft a box that can be filled with treasures or simply be on display as a reminder of a loving relationship with themselves . . . because our relationship with ourselves is the foundation of all the relationships in our lives.

Though simple in structure and easy to craft, a Self-Love Box can be a powerful tool of affirming the riches we each have within. After all, as Elisabeth Kübler-Ross said, "The ultimate lesson all of us have to learn is unconditional love, which includes not only others but ourselves as well."

Inner Inquiries for Journaling and Reflection

✳ What colors and images symbolize self-love to me? Why? If I could create a single saying or mantra to express self-love, what would it be?

✳ What would I most like someone to say to me? Can I say that same thing to myself?

"Things I Love" Pocket Tote Bag

The wonderful thirteenth-century Sufi poet Rumi wrote: "This is a subtle truth: Whatever you love, you are." This sage saying vibrates with truth because we can tell so much about a person when we learn what they love—someone who loves bird-watching, for instance, and who can identify birds according to their song, possesses a different energy than someone who loves to skydive.

The same is true of ourselves, of course, and sometimes we can muster up more self-regard when we take the time to catalog what it is in life we simply love. Is it the color orange, frog figurines, skiing in Colorado, "big band" music, programs on the Food Network, Norman Rockwell paintings? Or lush English gardens, classical music, King Charles Cavalier spaniels, vintage aluminum cups, Chinese celadon pottery, and *Breaking Bad* re-runs? You see the difference—each specific item that we love says something about us, about what inspires us, stimulates us, excites us, relaxes us.

Why not let the world get a sense of who we are—and give ourselves a dose of healthy self-appreciation—by advertising the kaleidoscope of our many loves through a "Things I Love" pocket tote? You may have seen something similar before—at the height of the scrapbooking craze, manufacturers made tote bags with photo pockets into which you could slip a favorite snapshot. This is the same idea, but amplified—not just photos of the people you love, but the *things* you love and, if they're small enough, perhaps even the objects themselves!

If you're not particularly good with a sewing machine, you can simply embellish an existing photo tote with postcards, dried flowers, ticket stubs, charms (and of course photos of loved ones)—anything that brings you joy and shows the world who you are! If working with fabric is part of your creative repertoire, then consider making your own pocket tote using transparent materials or even clear plastic or photo-protector pages. (A variation of this theme could also be to upload images of your favorites to your computer, then print them on photo-transfer paper that is ironed onto your tote, giving you an unchangeable but no less individualistic "picture" of who you are.)

By literally carrying around what it is we find beautiful, we can't help but be reminded of the beauty that we *are*. As the spiritual teacher Eckhart Tolle reminds us, "When you look upon another human being and feel great love towards them, or when you contemplate beauty in nature and something within you responds deeply to it, close your eyes for a moment and feel the essence of that love or that beauty within you, inseparable from who you are, your true nature. The outer form is a temporary reflection of what you are within, in your essence. That is why love and beauty can never leave you."

Inner Inquiries for Journaling and Reflection

* From the sublime to the ridiculous, what is it that I love? What colors, places, foods, music, experiences, people, programs, art pieces? What inspires me, and what "feels" like me?

* Based on that list, what does that tell me about who I am? Does looking over that list help me to appreciate myself more?

COLLAGED ARTIST TRADING CARDS

Looking at Ronnie McCullough's collage card, one can see the threads that have led to the fully realized tapestry of her career today. On the right side of the card is a cutout of a shy schoolgirl who looks longingly toward the card's center. Dressed all in white and carrying a large red clutch, she looks awkward, even rigid in her stance. The center images are large and confident: a full-length (and full-bodied) Marilyn Monroe looks down at a crowned headshot of Audrey Hepburn, both figures surrounded by rows upon rows of women in swimsuits. As Ronnie explains it, "This card represents my growing up as a plain Jane and my obsession with Hollywood's glamorous images."

In my own explorations of what "glamour" and beauty mean, and in following my passion for creative expression, I have been fortunate enough to meet fascinating men and woman whose livelihood is dedicated to helping women to express themselves as the living works of art that they are. I have met photographers who only take pictures of women and specialize in making their subjects look—and feel—like a goddess. I've met a woman who hand-paints, from scratch, a palette of colors she feels best enhances the essence of the person before her. Others I've met use fabric swatches to illustrate the best hues for bringing one's beauty forward. And it was on this journey that I met Ronnie, who, with a business partner, now makes her living as a makeover consultant—someone who, as her business tagline states, specializes in "the outward expression of your inner spirit—integrate what you wear with who you are."

For Ronnie, working with collage cards has been a powerful self-exploration and self-love tool. She explains the beginning of her practice:

> I found this form in 2001, I think, by accident. I was at a scrapbooking store in the Santa Rosa mall, and there was a book on the subject. I couldn't believe I didn't know about it. There was an Internet address in the back of the book, which I copied down . . . and wow! I found a Yahoo group to join and started creating them right away. They're known as Artist Trading Cards (ATCs)—they were expressly for trading, not selling.
>
> At this time, I had been creating larger collage works, but had many small images that weren't usable for those. What I loved was the challenge to say something in a single playing-card sized format or a series of "cards" that was portable. I could take a box of ideas, a few magazines, and go sit in a coffee shop and make art! And the best thing was uploading them onto the group site and trading these originals with others done by artists from all over the world . . . it was like having grownup pen pals! I received art from the Netherlands, Spain, Australia, New Zealand, and Canada as well as all over the United States. The size and that they be original works of art were the only rules. They could be in any medium. I made over 250 of these during one winter, sometimes staying in my PJs the whole day, hair uncombed, totally focused on this magical form.

Not only had Ronnie discovered a powerful medium, but also a global gathering—as she says, "Although it was the art form itself that first attracted me, I met a wonderful worldwide community of artists—and though I haven't stayed in touch, I still have my favorite pieces that I received from that time period."

Ronnie recommends this self-practice because, as she says, it's a format that is so easily accessible for anyone. In addition to her ATCs (which usually measure two-and-a-half by three-and-a-half inches), Ronnie likes to make SoulCollages®, a format pioneered in the late 1980s by Jean Houston. It was further refined and popularized by Seena B. Frost, who wrote a book—*SoulCollage® Evolving: An Intuitive Collage Process for Self-Discovery & Community*—and trained people to become certified facilitators of the process.

The SoulCollage® cards are usually created in a five-by-eight-inch format, but Ronnie likes to use old greeting-card stock, so her work is a little bit smaller—four-and-a-half by six-and-a-half inches.

One series Ronnie did used the size and format of playing cards—each card she made could be viewed from either side. She explains:

> I had an incredibly fun journey doing this series. It took me back to my girl-hood in the fifties. I loved the playing-card format that allows for right-side up and upside down, using very tiny details to create a whole. Unexpected figures appeared during the process, and looking at them now gives me a new appreciation for the milieu of the Hollywood glamour I grew up in, not knowing that it would lead to a career in which I act as fairy godmother to

women who haven't yet discovered their true beauty. I have a number of Soul Collage® cards that fit this theme.

For Ronnie, art and craft making as a spiritual practice has been a cherished pastime for decades. She sees her collage cards as an outlet that not only promote self-love, but also love of the Divine Feminine:

> I've been doing art as a spiritual practice since 1981 when I discovered collage and people who approached it with no rules—very different from my years in grammar and high school. I had no confidence in my ability to express anything of substance through art until I was 39. Early in my parenting of my five children I decided that they were not going to suffer as I did, so we raised them to know that they were artists from the get-go and treated them as such.
>
> They didn't all come away unscathed, however. My eldest was told in a high school career class that she couldn't choose art because she would never make any money at it. My third daughter's sketchbook was confiscated in third grade because she had drawn nudes and someone reported her. I imagine each one has at least one similar story to share, so as a society we still denigrate art as a viable path for young people to choose.

But art as a viable path for anyone to choose as a spiritual practice is a different story. Ronnie continues: "I've always known I was expressing my feelings when I approached any kind of art, though there is a definite difference in what I call process art—expressing my inner world—and what I design for beauty/aesthetics, though I might not know which world I have chosen until the piece is complete."

Ronnie had several art shows of her collage work between 1999 and 2003. One comment by a woman who bought her art, Ronnie remembers, stayed with her:

> She said my piece reminded her of the French Revolution and took her on an amazing journey. There was nothing concrete that would take an observer there, but just the idea that my art could evoke such a journey was an epiphany for me.
>
> Another revelation is that without conscious effort, my pieces invariably convey an Asian or French influence or the artist Escher. As I began to analyze my work, I discovered that I often include a vortex or a feeling of looking through a kaleidoscope.

For Ronnie, it's a natural process:

> Expressing love through art seems natural. I think of it more as expressing the Divine or the kind of love where my art comes through spirit and I have no idea where it will take me. So, in all honesty, I have to say it's an outer expression of mostly unconscious aspects that come through. I allow myself to go with what makes my solar plexus sing and discard everything else.

Ronnie sees her current work as an image and makeover consultant as an art form: "Women provide the canvas for my current art, which is uncovering, midwifing, and awakening women to their innate and essential beauty and providing them with the tools to express this through the art of dress."

Working with found images of femininity helped Ronnie to more fully embrace the inherent beauty in herself and in all women—and that, perhaps, is the ultimate makeover goal for us all.

Inner Inquiries for Journaling and Reflection

* When I view modern advertising, what is my response to the feminine images it contains?

* How might I creatively work with these images to construct a positive opinion of my own beauty and the unique beauty of other women?

"The beginning of love is to let those we love be perfectly themselves, and not to twist them to fit our own image. Otherwise we love only the reflection of ourselves we find in them."

−THOMAS MERTON

Crafting a Practice

For people who are beginning their exploration of "process art," Ronnie recommends three authors who, she says, were extremely helpful in mentoring her expression:

Frederick Franck, who wrote *The Zen of Seeing: Seeing/Drawing as Meditation*; and Lucia Capacchione, author of *The Creative Journal: The Art of Finding Yourself*, *Visioning: Ten Steps to Designing the Life of Your Dreams*, *Recovery of Your Inner Child*, and other books who has a wonderful article, "Losing Yourself in the Divine," (luciac.com/losing-yourself-in-the-divine) which expresses my feeling while I am in the creative process so well. Finally, Clarissa Pinkola Estes, author of *Women Who Run with the Wolves*, has been wonderfully helpful, especially in her audio recording, "The Creative Fire."

Intention Photo Frame Bracelet

As I have written before, I seem to have a mind that, upon spying something of interest, immediately starts to assess its usefulness as an art or craft supply, its ability to be transformed into something symbolic or meaningful. Such was the case when flipping through a friend's catalog of direct-sales jewelry from a company formerly known as Cookie Lee. I wanted to support my friend's new business, but I wasn't having much luck finding something I really wanted—until I spied a bracelet made of two parallel aurora borealis crystal strands, with six tiny silver plate picture frames, each measuring three-quarters of an inch high and one-half inch wide, circling it. The instructions on each little frame said to "Insert Photo Here," but I saw greater possibilities for this bracelet—to use it as a wearable collage of the intentions I wanted to keep before me.

At the time, I was self-employed as a spiritual director and creativity coach, struggling to create a successful business. That was the intention behind the photo of a Chinese red envelope (symbolizing good luck), with large-denomination greenbacks tucked within it. After using a photocopier to reduce that image (and others I found to represent my intentions) to less than one inch, I placed these miniature pictures into each frame on the bracelet. Other images I chose included a lighthouse, to remind myself to shine my light so all who were meant to be served by me would find me; a footprint in the sand, to call to mind the famous faith poem about being carried by God even when we can't see it; and a silhouette of someone with outstretched arms on a beach illumined by the citrus hues of a beautiful sunset to prompt me to keep in touch with the feelings of joy that I wanted (and want still) to embody.

Placing it on my wrist again more than a decade later, my Intention Photo Frame Bracelet still has resonance for me. Though my career (and thus some of my intentions) has changed with the passing years, I still find it empowering to look at the tiny images and remember what they meant to me. I appreciate the person I once was: she decided to keep her resolutions before her at all times. Like a portable vision board, my Intention Photo Frame Bracelet served to inspire me and keep me focused on that which I hoped to manifest in my life—not the least of which was a sense of self-appreciation for who I was as a person and the gifts I had to give as a professional. I am so happy to write I feel that self-appreciation now. Who knows how large a part my bracelet played in that?

If you like this idea of making a bracelet (or necklace) containing small photo frames into which you can place small pictures that depict your intentions, a search on the Internet will yield a number of sources where you can find them. You could make a bracelet or necklace for a single intention or one that represents several, as mine did. Simply fill the frames with reduced-size images that will remind you of what you hope to manifest in your life—fulfilling the words of Dieter Uchtdorf: "What we love determines what we seek, what we seek determines what we think and do, what we think and do determines what we become."

Inner Inquiries for Journaling and Reflection

✳ If I were to choose six different intentions that feel the most compelling for me right now, what would they be? Do they encompass all of my life or only a part of it (such as career)?

✳ Having just expressed those intentions in words, how would I "translate" them into images? For example, what single image would I choose to support an intention to eat more healthily and get more exercise?

"It is good to love many things, for therein lies the true strength, and whosoever loves much performs much, and can accomplish much, and what is done in love is well done."

–VINCENT VAN GOGH

"I Am" Affirmation Mandala

In some spiritual circles, it is said that the words "I Am" are the two most powerful words you can ever say—for what you choose to follow "I Am" shapes your reality. This is an important concept to grasp when looking at the subject of self-love, because too often the words we choose to follow "I am" are negative—as in, *I am fat*. Or *I am too old*. Or *I am not as talented as that person is*. Or whatever your particular phrase of *non*-self-love is.

Unless you've been camping in the woods for the last twenty years or so, you've no doubt come across magazine articles and TV programs that stress the importance of positive affirmations, "I am" statements that give you a sense of hope and possibility, rather than defeat and self-loathing. We may think we're protecting ourselves when we're being self-critical—that by saying those negative words to ourselves first, we're keeping ourselves from getting hurt or being judged—but science would not agree with you. Our self-talk is self-fulfilling, which is why the French psychologist Emile Coue promoted the daily mantra of "Every day, in every way, I'm getting better and better."

If Emile or Oprah haven't convinced you yet, let me try another approach. As a way of expressing self-love, one that uses your existing love of art and crafts, try working with your affirmations visually, by making an "I Am" Affirmation Mandala. A mandala is a square or circular shape whose interior is usually intricately patterned. Stemming from the Hindu and Buddhist traditions, mandalas are used as a tool for meditation, seen as an integrated view of wholeness. So, if your self-talk has tipped the balance and led you down a path of feeling decidedly un-whole, this could be an important project to try.

There are no rules, but I do have one suggestion for what to put in the center of your mandala: the words "I Am." If you're not yet able to muster up positive adjectives to follow, then list adjectives you *want* to embody. You will be listing these on separate pieces of paper, then cutting each affirmation into a strip, then pasting them around your "I Am" like rays of sunshine. "I am capable" could be one ray. "I am a lifelong learner" could be another. If you prefer, you can think of your Affirmation Mandala as a flower—with the seeds being the "I Am" and the petals being your affirmations.

Try to stay away from nouns unless they're similar to the example above ("I am a lifelong learner"). The point of this exercise is to celebrate the essence of who you are, not your roles in life. If you really get stuck, ask your friends and family members to help out by listing positive attributes they see in you. Of course, you can always include Dr. Coue's, because every day in every way you *are* getting better and better, especially if you use this Affirmation Mandala the way it's intended to be used—as a tool for contemplation and a symbol of your wholeness. As you proceed, remember these words from Goethe: "Love does not dominate; it cultivates." Cultivate the beautiful flower that you are by listing the many ways in which you bloom!

> "Looking back over a lifetime, you see that love was the answer to everything."
>
> —RAY BRADBURY

Inner Inquiries for Journaling and Reflection

✳ What grade would I give the quality of my self-talk? Do I get a passing grade or is it time for some remedial work?

✳ What would I like to embody? Whom do I personally admire and what qualities do they have that I would like to reflect? How does it feel when I list that quality after the words "I Am"?

The Love Language of Flowers

If you decide to do your "I Am" Affirmation Mandala in the shape of a flower, then the following flowers—all associated with love—may be good ones to use. While you're perusing the list, consider this: we often look to our romantic partners as being the appropriate ones to give us the gift of flowers, but why not treat yourself to a single stem or an assorted bouquet of blooms that says "I love you" to you?

Agapanthus: Love letters, love

Ambrosia: Reciprocated love

Bird of Paradise: Magnificence

Blue Violet: Faithfulness

Calla Lily: Magnificent beauty

Camellia (red): "You're a flame in my heart."

Camellia (white): "You're adorable."

Carnation (pink): A mother's love, a woman's love, "I'll never forget you."

Carnation (white): Innocence, faithfulness, pure love

Chrysanthemum (white): Truth, loyal love

Daffodil (in bunch): Joy, happiness

Forget-Me-Not: True love, hope

Gardenia: Joy, sweet love, "You're lovely."

Hibiscus: Delicate beauty

Hyacinth (blue): Constancy

Iris: Faith, hope, wisdom, "Your friendship means so much to me."

Lavender: Devotion

Lily of the Valley: Return of happiness, sweetness

Orange Blossom: Purity, innocence, eternal love

Orchid: Rare beauty, love, refinement

Ranuculus: "You are radiant with charm."

Rose: Love, passion, perfection

Sweet Pea: Lasting pleasure, "I think of you."

Zinnia (white): Goodness.

"You, yourself, as much as anybody in the entire universe, deserve your love and affection."

—BUDDHA

115

CRAFTING LOVE:
OTHERS IN THE WORLD

Chapter 6:

CRAFTING LOVE:
OTHERS IN THE WORLD

HERE'S WHERE THE RUBBER CAN MEET THE ROAD: TAKING the time to create a little treasure and freely distributing it into the world, usually not knowing the recipient but loving them anyway—loving them as a fellow human being on the path who deserves the sweet surprise of being gifted with something serendipitous. Sometimes we are witness to their delight, but most often we are not. We are simply the vehicle through which compassion—love—is expressed.

There's a whole movement developed around this idea. Many people are bonding together in "Art Abandonment" collectives (you can find groups on Facebook and other social-media sites) and posting photos of the art they leave for some lucky discoverer to find. There are also growing numbers of people who practice "craftivism"—using their art and crafts as a way of doing good in the world.

It is said that the Universe is always speaking to us, if only we had the eyes to see and the ears to hear. By crafting love for strangers, by making—and giving—little parts of ourselves for others to discover in their own Divine timing, we contribute to the magic of the world, and we contribute to the meaning of our lives—embodying the words of poet William Wordsworth, who wrote that they are "…that best portion of a good [wo]man's life, His little, nameless, unremembered acts/of kindness and of love."

"The best love is the kind that awakens the soul and makes us reach for more, that plants a fire in our hearts and brings peace to our minds."

—NICHOLAS SPARKS

POLYMER CLAY POCKET CHARMS

"Have a heart" carries a whole new meaning when it's said by Danna Schmidt, a celebrant and a ceremonialist, which, she says, "is a fancy way of saying that people pay me to craft love through custom-designed ceremonies across the lifespan from birth to earth." Danna loves to make tiny polymer clay hearts that she stamps with love words and designs. As she explains:

> I carry and give them away as pocket charms, have crafted hundreds of them for Celebrations of Life, and have been using them, more recently, as a pre-visit intention/invocation ritual for my hospice visits as well as a post-visit, self-care, and release ritual. I hold the charms in the palm of my hand and I reflect, to begin, on what I want to focus on with my patient. Afterwards, I meditate on the gift the visit gave me, any new insights I gleaned, and anything I need to let go of—like last Friday, when I accidentally tripped over a patient's medical air mattress on the floor and inadvertently tripped the alarm for the nurse to come running. Loving my bonehead self despite not having a clue what I'm doing!

Despite Danna's lighthearted story of release, she sees these little hearts as playing an important function:

> Gary Chapman asserts that there are five love languages: gifts, quality time, words of affirmation, acts of service and physical touch. Crafting love is my way of being multi-lingual and speaking all five love languages at once.
>
> Like most (or perhaps even all) artists, I have a loud critic in my head who always has a lot to say about the quality or lack thereof in my work. I began to notice, however, that when I turned my art into spiritual dedications to loved ones or to the unknown, Sacred Other, I began to silence the voice of the inner critic. This was my first conscious awareness of making that integral shift from head to heart in my art-making. This transformation began for me about five years ago and since then, I know of no other way to enter into my creative endeavors but to begin from and immerse myself in Heart while crafting.

If you, too, would like others to "have a heart," polymer clay hearts are easy to make, in any size you choose—though, if you want them to be pocket tokens, smaller will be better. You can find polymer clay in a rainbow of colors at your local craft store or online that can be "fired" in a toaster oven used as a kiln. (Please note: You do *not* want to use this same oven for food preparation. Consider buying a separate toaster oven dedicated to this use if you anticipate doing a lot of work in polymer clay.) There are also clays available that will air-dry. Once ready, you can sprinkle your little hearts wherever you go . . . and experience firsthand what it means to spread the love!

Inner Inquiries for Journaling and Reflection

* If I decided to make and give away little pocket charms, what shape(s) would I use, and why?

* How do I show my feelings of caring to those who are in my life? To strangers?

> "What we have once enjoyed, we can never lose. All that we love deeply becomes a part of us."
>
> —HELEN KELLER

Crafting a Practice

"I would invite others to treat their art and their craft as commissioned work because that is truly what it is. The divine High Commissioner, in all matters of heart, soul and art-making, is and always will be one's own heart.

"When I approach my work in this kind of intentional way, beginning with a word, phrase, feeling, or theme of what it is I wish my piece to illuminate in dedication to a specific Other, then magic occurs. I recognize that I am suddenly devoting my expressive attention to a larger purpose. While my creations will never be featured in the Sistine Chapel, I consider them to be my little altars I bequeath the world. My process is my own unique genuflection.

"So, I would counsel others to live the Rumi poem, which I think perfectly encapsulates the creative pilgrimage:

> *This is love; to fly toward a secret sky,*
> *to cause a hundred veils to fall each moment.*
> *First to let go of life.*
> *Finally, to take a step without feet.*

"This, too, is the process of crafting love: being willing to apprentice yourself to the unknown, privileging process over product, and embracing the beauty of creativity as both divine birth rite and liturgical rite.

"I don't have an artist's statement per se but if I did, it would be wrapped up in another Rumi quote about taking down an instrument, letting the beauty I love be what I do, and affirming my own thousand ways to kneel and kiss the ground. This quote, to me, truly embodies what it means to intertwine creative and spiritual practice. Crafting brings me as close as I get to kneeling at the altar of Creator energy, which is why I refer to this creative time and space as *altar*ed moments and affectionately name my creations as my 'little altars everywhere.'

"As someone who tends to go the extra mile in making heartfelt gifts for others, to the extent that my gifts often elicit the exclamation, 'Wow! This must have taken you forever!'–I will admit that, in a sense, they are correct. Crafting love IS my way to suspend time and journey to the always and foreverland that is available to us in the here and now."

—Danna Schmidt

KINDNESS CARDS

I received it on the day I became ordained as a Unity minister. My friend Judy had dropped one of her signature "Kindness Cards" through the slot of a beautiful box placed in the church foyer for cards and gifts. The size of a standard business card, it is printed with arresting artwork on the front—from a central circle (is it the center of a flower? the iris of an eye? a cell in the bloodstream?) radiates petal-shaped spokes in shades of green, blue, red, and yellow. On the other side, these words are written, each sentence prefaced with a tiny heart: "You are loved. You are magnificent. You matter."

Judy Ranieri, an author, artist, and women's group facilitator, tells the story behind the card:

> This card was designed by a friend of mine, Tammy Jean Zoller—who went by "TJ." She had stage 4 breast cancer and passed away in 2013. This artwork represents how she experienced joy. I wanted to honor her life in some way and added the quotes on the back.
>
> The story behind the Kindness Cards started a number of years ago, when there was a lot of negative energy in the world, a lot of negative headlines, and I wanted to counteract that. So, I started to offer workshops on joy. TJ took one of my workshops. One of the things we did in it was defining what joy was for us, going through the senses—what does joy look like, feel like, taste like, sound like, and smell like? TJ did the piece of artwork that's on the card

and shared that for her, joy starts at a cellular level, and if she stayed with it at a cellular level, the more it expanded.

TJ was kind to everyone, and used to carry a bag—she called herself a "Sherpa"—filled with scientific books. She would pull out a book and read quotes, one of which was "Kindness increases wellbeing . . . and stress lowers wellbeing." So we talked about that, about how kindness is contagious, and that we could create a "kindness wave" that was important to keep going. TJ gave me the original artwork that's now on the front of the Kindness Cards. As a surprise, I made some cards up with her artwork on it, and she was so excited about them. I remember saying to her, "The world is going to know that you've been here."

I use these cards in many ways. I leave them for waiters and waitresses. I give them to the people in tollbooths. I put them on chairs at events I attend, without people knowing it's me. I put them on car windows, in our local Safeway parking lot, and in different locations in hospitals. I shared that I do this with members of a drumming and healing circle I belong to, and the next thing I knew, they wanted to participate! Over five thousand cards have been circulated and used in ways I never thought of. One person passed them out, anonymously, at a family reunion, while others had them sent back to the kitchen help in restaurants they frequented.

These cards have taken on a life of their own. I later made some other Kindness Cards on my own to make that kindness wave continue. I have created four other designs with different quotes on them, like "I See You With My Heart." Other people who are now doing the same thing have used different quotes, like "THANK YOU for your kindness and courtesy" and "You were noticed, appreciated, and made me smile."

I call them "Kindness Cards," but others call them "Magnificence Cards." What the cards are saying in essence is: I see you. I acknowledge you. And I appreciate you. Acknowledging people and letting them know that you *see* them is a practice of love.

Inner Inquiries for Journaling and Reflection

* ✳ What statement(s) would I most like to hear from the Universe? Would I like to feel that I'm seen?

* ✳ Do I really see the people around me? How have I shown or told others that I really see them?

"It matters not who you love, where you love, why you love, when you love, or how you love, it matters only that you love."

–JOHN LENNON

Crafting Your Own Kindness Cards

If you are interested in creating your own Kindness Cards, it's very simple. Depending on how you want to use them, you can either make your own—draw or paint on them, make a collage on them, handwrite your own sentiments—or, if you want them in large quantities, you can have them printed in standard business-card or postcard size.

If you're not sure what art to use on the front of your card, Judy has some ideas:

> If you want to make your own Kindness Cards, it's very easy to do. If you're not an illustrator, you can take a picture in nature and that becomes your original art. You can also take a photo of a quilt, pottery piece, collage that you've made—photographing even just a corner of it—and that becomes your art.
>
> Once you have selected the art for your card and know what sayings you want to put on the back, you're ready to have your Kindness Cards printed. There are many companies—local printing businesses or websites like MOO and Vistaprint—that will print your cards using an easy template. You just fill in the blanks with the words you want and upload your image for the other side!

POETRY EGGS

The day I first encountered the work of poet Dawn Trook was a day like any other . . . except that it wasn't. Parking in the driveway of the church I serve, my eyes spied something purple hidden in the large clay pot of an outdoor plant near our back door. What could it be? As I got closer, I saw it was a plastic Easter egg. On one side it had black writing spelling out "Great Egg Hunt. Year 3, Day 224." On the other side were these instructions: "Please open. Poem inside."

Living in an age in which hazardous materials have been packaged just as innocuously, I must confess that at first I wasn't sure if it was safe to open this little purple egg promising poetry. But my innate trust of the Universe and delighted sense of expectation took command of the situation, and open the egg I did—finding a folded piece of paper with this poem printed on it:

I Am From

A moving van every
three years a new
house never a home

Never a place
of belonging
from nowhere

I continue to roam
landing on
California shores

Roaming again
and again
To find my way

Being hunted to be
someone else
searching inward
to rest in my soul.

This poem—an appropriate poem to find in a potted plant outside a spiritual center—was followed by a name (Leslie Belleau-Sachs), a date (January 23, 2014), and this paragraph:

> This poem-filled egg is part of the Great Egg Hunt, a project started in California on April 26th, 2011. Every day in Merced, Santa Cruz, Modesto, or San Francisco (unless the egg goes somewhere farther away on vacation), a poem is placed in an egg and hidden somewhere. If you have found this egg-poem, please like the Great Egg Hunt on Facebook and share about your search/finding and, if you wish, pass it on and hide it for another to find. Year 3/Day 224.

Dawn Trook, a writer, musician, baker, actor, performer, and educator living in Merced, California—and the founder of the Great Egg Hunt—explains how it all came about:

> I dropped the eggs in Merced, where I lived for a year starting in April 2011. I got the idea right after Easter because I always have so much fun doing the egg hiding for my church egg hunt on Easter. I casually posted the idea on my Facebook page and forgot about it. But my boyfriend at the time saw it and said, "Why didn't you tell me you are going to hide a poem-filled Easter egg for a year?" So, then I felt like I had to do it!
>
> It became a little thing. The local paper wrote about it, and there was a small contingent of devoted hunters and a team of local poets writing and

hiding. [Clues to eggs' whereabouts were posted on the project website, greategghunt.blogspot.com.]

I teach English composition and creative writing at UC Merced and have been pretty devoted to literary community outreach work since I've been there. Some colleagues and I had talked about poetry "bombing" the community. This sort of came from that conversation. And then I wanted to follow through on the year commitment, even though that was a lot of creative pressure. After a year, a team of people in different cities started hiding poem-filled eggs on random days. I kind of hoped it would spread across the country, but the only one who kept up a weekly writing/hiding, was my mom [Leslie Belleau-Sachs, who wrote the poem in the egg I found], who's been doing it since 2012.

What I love about this project is that it's a leap of faith. We mostly never know if the egg is found or if the poem is read or appreciated. But we have some nice stories of the eggs being found. I saw a little boy in a mall playing with my egg one evening. I don't know if it was opened. An egg hunter in Merced interrupted someone's lunch to ask if he could have the egg sitting on the table. The guy who was eating lunch asked to read the egg-poem too, and then asked if he could keep it, because he thought it would speak to his daughter. That same devoted hunter found another guy cleaning a parking lot at a grocery store and asked if he had found the egg. The cleaner had, so the hunter asked if he could read the poem. He then took a photo with the parking lot cleaner who proudly held up his find. Someone last week said they remembered when a friend rather recklessly ran to the south side of town at 11:00 p.m. at night, which is not recommended, to retrieve an egg.

Though the project has waned with time, it isn't over easy. Dawn says, "I'm thinking about stuffing the eggs with famous people's poems, and picking up the project that way."

Don't you feel a sense of delight just reading about this project? That's how I felt upon opening my little egg, which sat underneath my computer monitor as part of the little altar I created for the writing of this book. Distributing your art randomly is a wonderful exercise in both courage and surrender because you don't know how it will be received. This kind of crafting is about showing love, not being lauded. Besides, as Plato taught, "At the touch of love, everyone becomes a poet."

Inner Inquiries for Journaling and Reflection

* How do I feel about the element of surprise?
* What would I have fun "abandoning" for someone else to find? Why is that particular thing meaningful to me?

HEALING HATS

My heart longs to knit, but I have learned through trial and error (mostly error) I will never be a knitter. I'm sad about that because there are so many ways knitting can be used in the service of others, as Jennifer Stover's story illustrates. Jennifer has seen her desire to use her preferred craft of knitting as a way to express love grow from creating knitted hats for people undergoing chemo treatments to a larger movement encompassing all kinds of knitted solace. She relates:

> I first learned how to knit from my mom, who taught me the two basic knitting stitches when I was 31 and had a one-year-old daughter. From that point on, I was passionate to learn everything else as fast as I could. A few months after learning how to knit, I saw in the local church bulletin that there was a group making chemo hats for local oncology units. I joined the very next week and haven't stopped since. Over eight years later, the charity-based group has increased in membership and gone from knitting and crocheting hats for oncology patients to making prayer shawls for hospitals, bereavement gowns for neonatal intensive care units, sending hats to orphanages and on mission trips, making washcloths for radiation patients, and donating hats, scarves, and money to the American Cancer Society Relay for Life annual event.
>
> From the very beginning I have always believed knitting or any type of craft can be a way of expressing love. I grew up in a family of artists; from

painting to sewing to crafting to gardening to singing, I have always been taught that time has always been an expression of love and sharing one's talents is giving of oneself and efforts are always appreciated, no matter how imperfect the outcome.

How I express love is quite amorphous throughout my knitting journey. I express love to my mom and friends by spending quality time when we knit together and share projects and patterns with each other. I express love to my family and friends by making handcrafted items for which I have personally chosen the yarn and the pattern to suit the individual. I express love when I knit for charitable causes, whether it be a bereavement gown for the NICU, a shawl given to a senior home or chaplain to pass out at a hospital, or a blanket given to a child at a foster home. This is my way of providing sympathy and compassion in the hopes that the items I make will provide peace and under-standing that someone is thinking and praying for them. I express love to strangers by allowing the opportunity to be receptive to conversations and interest while I'm knitting in public. I express love to students as I teach by sharing my knowledge and excitement to eager learners. I express love to myself by making quality time to learn and experience new techniques while enjoying the process of creating something for someone I love, whether they know me or not.

What advice would she give someone just starting a "Crafting Love" project? "Understand the reason why you're knitting," Jennifer counsels. "Is it out of want, obligation, education, necessity, or a desire to fill a void? There is nothing wrong with knitting for yourself or to only knit for charitable causes. It's when you knit because you 'have to' instead of because you want to that will lead to resentment of the craft and, in turn, resentment of others."

Jennifer adds, "Finding people to connect with—whether through a church, the neighborhood, at local yarn store, or in another group—is important. It helps fill a social need of acceptance, accountability, and guidance." She recommends the online knitting and crocheting resource Ravelry.com. It is described as "a community site, an organizational tool, and a yarn and pattern database for knitters and crocheters."

Jennifer's favorite charity-based knitting book is *Knit Along with Debbie Macomber: A Charity Guide for Knitters*. The book provides knitting patterns and includes worthy charities in need of items it lists.

In conclusion, Jennifer states:

> There is a saying in my charity group: A head for every hat. No matter what the size, color, or even mistake-filled project, items received are loved and appreciated. We have had many new people want to learn how to knit or crochet because they or a family member went through chemo and received a hat or blanket. They, in turn, wanted to pay it forward and learn how to make hats for future patients themselves.

My most treasured moments in knitting are when I teach children. I love planting that seed of accomplishment by instructing how to create fabric with two sticks and some string and watching their eyes shine when the mechanics make sense. I love when I ask them what they want to make. Three out of four times, kids will mention they want to make something for their sibling or mother or grandmother. Kids have a genuine need for love and to show love. By giving them another tool to help them accomplish that and bond with an older generation gives me a sense of accomplishment.

If you want to use your knitting skills to make healing hats or blankets (and after reading Jennifer's story, who wouldn't be?), try an Internet search to see if there are groups already in place in your community who could use your help. If not, a book like the one Jennifer recommended or researching national organizations may yield an outlet. It aids in someone's healing process and will help you too. As Karl Menninger once expressed it, "Love cures, the ones who receive love and the ones who give it, too."

Inner Inquiries for Journaling and Reflection

* If I were to come up with a slogan personally analogous to "a head for every hat," what would it be? "Food for every bowl?" "School for every child?" What social issue or need do I care most about?

* What crafting tool/activity would I most love to share with children?

Healing Colors

Should you decide to craft a polymer clay pocket charm, knit a healing hat, or do some other form of artistic outreach, it might be helpful to know what colors are commonly thought to have healing characteristics. Here's a list of effects that certain colors are said to have on healing:

Blue: Good for calming the mind and cooling the body (reducing fevers). Some feel it helps with healing burns. Blue is thought to be good for eliminating headache pain and reducing high blood pressure. In Chinese medicine, it is the healing color of the kidneys.

Green: Green is considered valuable for easing the ability to breathe and helping the lungs and heart. Some consider green to be a prime healing color in general, helping with tissue regrowth and mending broken bones. In Chinese medicine, green is the healing color of the liver.

Orange: Creates balance, increases immunity and sexual potency, and helps in shock or trauma situations to provide clarity and calmness. Orange also helps with chest and kidney diseases as well as digestive ailments.

Purple or Violet: Useful for emotional problems as it promotes calm and inner peace. It is also said to help with rheumatism and epilepsy, reducing pain, and healing bones.

Red: It is counseled to use red sparingly, but this color is said to assist with the healing of burns, cuts, and infections. Sometimes called the "antibiotic" of color energy, in Chinese medicine red is the healing color of the heart.

Yellow: Suitable for assisting with mental clarity as well as for skin problems, nerves, kidneys, and liver. Yellow is the healing color of the spleen in Chinese medicine.

White: Some consider white to be the best reliever of pain and a purifying color. In Chinese medicine, white is the healing color of the lungs.

"Love is a fruit in season at all times,
and within reach of every hand."

—MOTHER TERESA

KNITTED BEARS

Placed in a box together, their expressions are inviting and sweet—little "mother bears," knitted from yarn. Each one individual, like real mothers are: there is a brown one with long brown yarn hair tied into pigtails with fuchsia bows; a black one, dressed in red, with the happiest of stitched smiles; a gray one, dressed in yellow yarn and adorned with a jaunty rainbow-striped scarf. Their creator, Melissa Rodgers, describes herself as having been "a compulsive creative" her whole life, who especially loves making things for others: "It seems like I've always used my craft as a way of expressing love." Even as a child, she would make toys and dolls for her little sister. "I have been crafting ever since I was old enough to work with any kind of materials," Melissa remembers. "Probably around age two or three, and have never stopped. The spiritual angle behind my crafting probably didn't begin until early adulthood, when I began to feel a strong need to connect with something greater than myself."

Melissa continues:

> I think I'm a nurturer at heart but a fairly reserved person overall, so creating is a very quiet way to give of myself. I had a very dear friend in junior high and high school who supported me steadfastly through my parents' divorce and my mother's early death. My way of giving to him was to make a Raggedy Andy. Something one doesn't usually do for a teenage boy, I suspect!
>
> As a young mother, I created a Christmas-tree skirt with appliques of my

children's handprints on it for each year. It was a visible expression of how much I loved watching them grow. Now in their twenties, they still remember it fondly.

Over time, seeing how much people appreciate handmade items, I've tried to make a point of always making at least one Christmas gift for each member of my immediate family. I do the same for my staff at work—always some small handmade thing. This past Christmas, it was an embroidered bookmark. Nothing big but something that takes time, thought and effort to show how much I appreciate each one of them.

Melissa describes how her making of the sweet little Mother Bears began:

I recently had the gift of a six-week recovery period from surgery and decided to focus on crafting for a cause. Upon reviewing a number of charity knitting options, I settled on the Mother Bear Project (motherbearproject.org). Their home page indicated: "The Mother Bear Project is dedicated to providing comfort and hope to children affected by HIV/AIDS in emerging nations, by giving them a gift of love in the form of a hand-knit or crocheted bear. The simple gift of a hand-knit bear with a tag signed by the knitter has touched children with the message that they are unconditionally loved."

As a doll crafter from way back, I was immediately hooked. Seeing the hundreds of pictures of bears with their new little friends just sealed the deal and I started crocheting. Seventeen bears later, I'm still going strong and aiming to complete the alphabet this year.

The organization has distributed over 139,000 bears since 2003. Truly amazing in so many ways!

Melissa's desire to touch children's lives doesn't stop there. She says:

Another bit of work I really love is teaching hand-sewing skills to kids, which came about quite by accident. My husband and I attend a few primitive skills gatherings each year, where one of the garments of choice is a *capote*—a blanket coat from the fur-trapper era. Oftentimes, there is someone there to teach *capote*-making but last fall, at Rabbitstick (an event that teaches primitive skills), there wasn't. Known for my needlework skills, I was sought out by a couple of nine- or ten-year-old boys who wanted to make their own coats. It's a long project, so I had my doubts, but they came with their own blankets so I couldn't possibly refuse! These young boys sat with me for at least three full days, stitching away, hardly taking a break even to eat. They stitched by hand—every seam. Keeping up with their energy just about wore me out, but the look on their faces when they went off proudly wearing their own hand-made coats was priceless. I was so happy for "my boys!"

The project closest to Melissa's heart these days is making the Mother Bears: "So far, I've crocheted fifteen bears—each one unique. Discovering this group has prompted such passion, joy, and sense of meaning. Plus, through the related Ravelry group, I've connected with a whole community of amazingly creative women. The care, love and originality poured into the bears is remarkable—and such an inspiration."

Through the knitting of toy bears for children in other countries, Melissa has not only found a cause and a calling, she's also found a community. Whether you choose Melissa's form of outreach or find another outreach project that touches your heart, the important thing is just to begin. When we talk about "crafting love" for others, as Jerome Cummings reminds us, "Love is shown in your deeds, not in your words."

Inner Inquiries for Gratitude and Reflection

✳ Is there an organization I'm drawn to that uses a form of crafting for outreach? If not, what causes are close to my heart?

✳ How can I create a greater sense of community through my crafting?

Crafting a Practice

Melissa Rodgers offers more advice:

Just start! Don't worry about "not being creative" and certainly don't worry about perfection. Time is a precious commodity in this day and age, spending it on others is priceless.

Try to find something that speaks to you as a creative soul, something that helps you grow. Have fun. Experiment. Pick up an inspirational book, like *Crafting Calm* or *A String and a Prayer.* [Author's note: Melissa happened to mention two books I wrote!] Those two books were a landmark for me. I also scour magazines such as *Spirituality and Health* and *Where Women Create* for ideas and inspiration.

I've only recently come to realize that crafting for wellness and personal growth is my calling, so I am currently exploring opportunities to share more formally and deliberately with others by teaching classes and leading workshops.

And explore the history of how people have infused creativity into their everyday lives. Look at folk art, ethnic dress, patchwork quilts, cooking . . . the list is endless. Art can be almost anything.

CRAFTING LOVE:
THE DIVINE

Chapter 7:

CRAFTING LOVE: THE DIVINE

> "From a spiritual perspective, each individual heart is a place where Divine love is expressed and experienced. That's what it's designed for. That love shows up in an unlimited number of shapes and sizes, colors and flavors. We are here to love, as big and as fearlessly as we possibly can."
> – JEFFREY R. ANDERSON

THIS IS WHERE LOVE BEGINS AND ENDS. NO MATTER WHAT our name is for it—the Universe, the Divine, Spirit, God—when we tap into it we know that it is a Source beyond us, it is truly the capital-M Mystery. And it is from this Source—from the Creator—that we create; no matter what our personal theology is, if we believe we are expressions of the Divine, then by definition we are inherently creative.

For me, and for many others, the relationship between creativity and spirituality is not only intertwined, but two faces of the same stirring in the heart. I believe this so passionately that I host a radio show on Unity.fm called *Creative Spirit*, on which I interview artists and craftspeople about what they see as and how they express this connection between art and soul. Of course, what's infused in all of it is love—a love that rushes like a river after spring rain, becoming one with everything in its path.

It's also a way to feel connected to our Source—to transcend the mundane and experience the miraculous. The musician Prince put it this way: "To create something from nothing is one of the greatest feelings . . . I wish it upon everybody. It's heaven."

"Your task is not to seek for Love, but merely to seek and find all the barriers within yourself that you have built up against it."

—RUMI

"When we love, we always strive to become better than we are. When we strive to become better than we are, everything around us becomes better too."

—PAOLO COEHLO

COILED RAG BASKETS

They come in every color you can imagine, a seemingly endless spiral of soft coils in beautiful, repurposed fabric that are sometimes lidded and adorned with a special button top. One in shades of lavender, purple, and periwinkle has a lid crowned with a purple-enamel flowers. Another basket is made in earthen colors of umber and ochre and topped with a concave wooden slab. Eastery pastel shades of spring green and pale yellow are combined for a third adorned with an unpainted round bead.

These are the coiled rag baskets of Donna Caldwell. They are perfect to use for holding written prayers or intentions. Donna has crafted all of her life—knitting, embroidery, cross-stitchery, cake decorating, and more—but became conscious of it being a spiritual practice within the last several years. For Donna, it takes only two words to describe what it's like when she makes these beautiful love crafts: "Pure joy!"

For those who want to start crafting as a spiritual practice, Donna counsels: "Surrender all old beliefs and step into the now moment. You can't help but experience what you do as love, as God nurturing you in joyful ways." Talk of God comes naturally for Donna, who is a minister serving a Unity church in Castro Valley, California. She has made her coiled-rag baskets as fundraisers for her congregation, including an annual Easter-basket raffle. Donna fills her coiled-rag Easter baskets with holiday candies and gift certificates contributed by local merchants.

Donna remembers how she first came to basket making: "A dear friend of mine taught me how to make these baskets in 2014, and I just fell in love with the process. You never can tell how the pattern in the material will look once you cut it into strips and wrap it around the clothesline and sew it together. Basically, it is 'cloth pottery' shaped on the sewing machine instead of a potter's wheel."

If you are intrigued by this age-old craft of making a coiled basket, first consider what use you want the basket to have. Will it be used as a spiritual tool to place prayers or affirmations in? Will it be a container to carry something in, such as a journal, daily meditation books, or divination cards? Or will it be devoted to a particular holiday, like Donna's Easter baskets are?

Once you've decided on the basket's purpose, then appropriate cloth can be chosen for making the coils. You can pick a significant button or bead to make the handle if the basket will have a lid. Since the basket itself is a container, perhaps there's no better way to contain our sense of the love all around us!

Inner Inquiries for Journaling and Reflection

* Do I see any relationships between my favorite craft or art activity and another (such as Donna's baskets being "cloth pottery")?

* What surprises do I find in the making of my own craft or art? What aspect of it is unknowable until I've finished?

Crafting a Coiled Rag Basket

Donna offers the following instructions for those who would like to explore making coiled rag baskets:

All you need to make cloth pottery is a sewing machine that has a zigzag stitch, fabric cut into three-quarter-inch-wide strips, three-sixteenth-inch cotton clothesline, and thread that matches your fabric. Wrap the fabric around the clothesline and sew it into a coil on the machine. Then lift the sewn coil and continue sewing to make the sides of the pottery.

If you want further instruction, look for books about "sewing pottery" or "sewing baskets" or "sewing bowls." (It's all the same thing.)

GODDESS ROSARIES

I remember when I first saw them, how captivating they were in their beauty and diversity: a small silver angel flying on a strand of cloud-blue angelite; a large Our Lady of Guadalupe strung with amethyst beads and silver spacers in the shape of her roses; three clay Venus of Willendorf figurines, perfectly punctuating a strand of smooth black beads separated by irregularly shaped clear quartz nuggets; a Quan Yin clothed in warm colors, accompanied by peach-colored pearls. These represent just a few of Jennifer Mantle's Goddess Rosaries, which serve to do the same thing the name of her Etsy shop—Adore Her Designs—suggests: Adore Her.

Jennifer remembers when she made her first Goddess Rosary:

> The first rosary I made was an experiment, a listening to my inner knowing with curiosity, to see if this seemingly random phrase had any meaning for me. The phrase "goddess rosary" appeared in my consciousness while I was studying Women's Spirituality at Sophia University. The words led me on a truly magical journey, including finding a community I adore and a little side business of selling them that allows me to connect with my customers, my intuition, the Divine and with crystals. How magical is that!

For Jennifer, crafting is a way of life. In fact, she says:

I can't remember *not* crafting! Explicitly doing so as a spiritual practice began in my teens, when my church youth group leader had us make collages in group. I have never stopped making arts and crafts of some form or another as part of my spiritual exploration and expression.

The crafts that I do now—painting, collaging, art journaling, and beading—began out of a need to do them, a need to have my hands engaged in tangible acts of devotion and creation. I think that them being a form of expressing love of the Divine was always there as an undercurrent, but perhaps not something I articulated clearly until now!

For people who may not currently have an art or craft practice, Jennifer suggests to just *begin:*

The most important thing to do is to start. Whatever mode you choose, just do it. Let the laundry and the dishes wait—art-making won't wait. Give yourself ten or twenty minutes if that's all you can, and just make something. Train yourself to let go of the result—that's a byproduct. The act of crafting is the devotional practice that deserves your attention and that you deserve to engage in.

If you don't know where to start, or what calls to you, Jennifer suggests looking through printed materials and websites for inspiration. "I find lots of inspiration from women artists online," Jennifer says, "particularly on Pinterest and Instagram as well as teachers I know in person and follow through other social-media outlets."

It's more than just a pastime, Jennifer says:

> For me, art-making is a way of healing. Every stitch a knitter knits or brush-stroke on the canvas or bead on the strand contributes to the wholeness of the maker, the viewer, and the wearer. We are recreating ourselves as whole beings each time we take up our tools. The blessings of our creations multiply when a painting hangs on the wall of a loved one, a new baby is wrapped in a handmade blanket, when a beaded treasure is gifted from mother to daughter. The world needs your art! Set it free!

Inner Inquiries for Journaling and Reflection

* Where do I find my sources of inspiration? Where might I find more—in a bookstore "crafts" section, in an art museum, in groups of like-minded crafters on social media?

* If I were to make a rosary or prayer beads depicting my conception of the Divine, what would the main figure be? What materials and colors would I choose?

Deities Who Symbolize Love

While most deities in world religions represent the fullness of Divine love, some are associated with human love more than others. Here are a few of them:

Aphrodite (Greek) is of course one of the most well-known deities of love, and further represents beauty and sexuality.

Bastet (Egyptian), the cat goddess, is not only the goddess of felines, but also of beauty, dance, love, and perfume.

Freyja (Norse) is a goddess associated with beauty and love, magic and shamanism—but also with war and death.

Oshun (Yoruba) is the goddess of beauty, intimacy and love, and also represents diplomacy and wealth. She is associated with fresh water, and sometimes is depicted as a mermaid.

Parvati (Hindu) is the Hindu goddess most associated with love as well as devotion and fertility. Though gentle, she represents qualities of the Mother Goddess—the most powerful of all deities.

Xochiquetzal (Aztec)—her name means "precious feather flower"—is a goddess associated with beauty, fertility, and female power. In addition to being a patroness of pregnancy and childbirth, she is also a patroness of crafts traditionally practiced by women such as embroidery and weaving!

Spiritual Rhythm Paintings

For painter Westy Faison, expressing himself through paint is something he's done almost his whole life. But painting as a spiritual practice and as a way of expressing love had its own schedule: "It was sudden," Westy remembers. "I saw Sesshu's 'Splashed Ink Landscape,' painted in Japan, in the fifteenth century. The picture contains only the essential or 'divine nature' of the view. Sesshu seems to have released it from his own spirit by way of brush and ink. I immediately wanted to paint like that."

Westy remembers his process of turning workaday efforts into sacred art: "First, I painted with brush and ink after reading *On the Laws of Japanese Painting* by Henry P. Bowie. I still seek similar effects, but now I use acrylic paint. I focus on a sense of rhythm and motion while I paint. This prevents an attachment to visual results. That attachment dampens the spiritual experience."

For those who would like to paint as a spiritual practice, to express their love of the Divine through their art, Westy has the following advice:

"Practice your craft," as singer/songwriter Ani Difranco answered someone seeking advice. The "divine" stuff happens only after mundane practice. Practice can be boring. But then creativity becomes something you do instead of an occasional inspiration.

I chose a career as a decorative painting contractor simply to keep a brush moving as much as possible. The twenty-five years of repetitive labor has paid

me back. I don't have to think too much about how to paint. It just happens.
I'm not always happy with the result, but the process moves itself.

For those recoiling inwardly at the thought of a disciplined practice, Westy has a story:

> I took two drawing workshops with the late Frederick Franck. The sessions
> were grueling: eight hours drawing and no talking. Lunch was silent! Frederick
> even playfully slapped my drawing hand when I lost focus on the drawing as a
> whole. I was focusing on details and trying to "make a picture." He wanted me
> to stay "scribbling" and staying in the "dance" of drawing. I sometimes invoke
> that incident to correct myself.
>
> My grandfather is the late S. Lane Faison. He was a great and influential art
> historian and art critic. Poppa praised one of my paintings. He felt viscerally
> that it had "guts." Many of my other paintings he said were just "exercises." I
> liked this for two reasons. One, I always appreciate praise that involves other
> senses—for example, when someone says "I can hear those waves," "I can feel
> it," et cetera. Second, in any spiritual or other practice, "gutsy" moves happen
> only after many "exercises."

For Westy, moving into the rhythm of painting is spiritual. It is a point at which something beyond himself takes over. While you might want to explore painting as a conduit
to this state, there are other ways to experience this kind of creative rhythm too. Try

experimenting with any craft you do—with knitting or writing poetry or working with clay. When do you feel that you have entered a rhythm beyond (and despite) yourself? As Westy counsels, don't worry about how good your work is or get attached to the results—approach it in the spirit of love. As Emmet Fox did: "I have chosen the path of Love. My own heart is to be my workshop, my laboratory, my great enterprise, and love is to be my contribution to humanity."

Inner Inquiries for Journaling and Reflection

* What craft do I "practice"? What is my philosophy around the concept of practice?

* When have I felt "rhythm" when creating? What ingredients of my environment or process led up to that feeling of being in rhythm? Did it feel like a transcendent or spiritual state?

"I have decided to stick with love.
Hate is too great a burden to bear."
—MARTIN LUTHER KING, JR.

Magic Wands

Most of us grew up under the influence of *The Wonderful World of Disney*—and for many of us, "wonderful" translated to "magical." We placed the fantasy and the color and the pixie dust under the umbrella of Magic. Who among us, boy and girl, *didn't* want to have a magic wand? When we were children and thought about magic, it had a pure, enchanting quality that lived up to the acronym that some adults still use to define it: *Manifesting All Good in Consciousness.*

What better way to manifest all good in consciousness than by crafting a tool of the trade—a magic wand? For Jeanine Byers, an intuitive and spiritual coach living in Savannah, Georgia, crafting "magic wands" is a powerful way to express love for the Divine and all the magic of life. She remembers:

> When my son was born fourteen years ago, I began scrapbooking every moment of his life that I could capture. I didn't want to miss a thing! But I didn't start crafting wands as part of my spiritual practice until about three or four years ago.
>
> I was shifting away from patriarchal Christianity, and decided I needed a mother god. I think I was reading a book or watching a video that told me I'd need a magic wand as I entered this brave new world. So, I created one. I gathered some wood, chose my crystals and ribbons, and made my first wand. After that, I was hooked. Making wands became a part of

that work. They felt (and still feel) so wonderful in my hands: Powerful. Empowering.

Jeanine realized how significant the practice could be: "Crafting the wands not only enabled me to express love but deepened my spiritual connection with the Divine. I noticed a profound sense of connection and love every time I held them. They all connected me to the energy of love."

Interestingly, Jeanine notes, each of her wands has a distinct "feeling," a different emotional connection: "My faerie wand has light energy and makes me feel happy. My priestess wands feel strong and powerful when I hold them. And my goddess wand feels so gentle and soft it calms me just to hold it in my hand. I crafted them in love, and the crafting part of my experience is long over, but the loving relationship continues."

If you're intrigued by the possibilities of crafting wands as a spiritual practice, Jeanine suggests weaving it into what you already do: "If you begin with prayer or lighting a candle, you could do that first and then begin the crafting. You can also set a strong intention as you begin, that the crafting you are about to do be infused with love and connection." Isn't that what we want for all our art and crafts? Because it is that love and connection that is truly magical.

> "You are the Soul of the Soul of the Universe, and your name is Love."
> —RUMI

Inner Inquiries for Journaling and Reflection

✳ What do I think of when I hear the word "magic?" Does it bring me joy, delight, the infinite sense of possibility that I felt when I was a child?

✳ If I were to craft a magic wand for a particular intention, what would it be? What in my life right now most calls for a little bit of "magic"– manifesting all good in consciousness?

"Every movement, every glance, every thought and every word can be infused with love."

–THICH NHAT HANH

"Love is the real work of your life. It is your spiritual path. It is the key to your growth and evolution."

–ROBERT HOLDEN

SACRED HEART NICHOS

It seems only fitting that the last craft listed in a book titled *Crafting Love* utilizes the universal symbol for love—the heart. This symbol is given as a token of love not only in the Western hemisphere but also in the East. One of my treasured possessions is a little handmade heart necklace that was given to me in China. Hung on a pink silk cord, this little stuffed heart is made of bright yellow-and-red velvet, with a sequin and star on each side affixed by a seed bead. At the bottom is a yellow silk tassel connected to the heart by a short strand of pearlescent green beads. Holding it in my hands, I will always remember the kind woman who gave it to me, and the hospitality she demonstrated in every action when I was a guest in her house, located in a rural area outside of Xian.

But creating a nicho—or shadow box—in the shape of a heart goes one step further: it is a powerful way to express your love for the Divine. Nichos are especially ubiquitous in Latin cultures. Due to the prevalence of Catholicism, portrayals of the Sacred Heart—which represent Christ's Divine Love for humanity (depictions of the Virgin Mary's Sacred Heart can also be found)—are seen adorning everything from jewelry to wall-hangings. Because of their popularity, it has become very easy to find a ready-made Sacred Heart nicho, usually made of tin and in many different sizes, on Mexican folk-art gallery websites, Etsy, and eBay.

Alternatively, if you have trouble finding one already made or one big enough for all you want to include, you can always try making a nicho yourself. I have made three-dimensional shrines out of things like a hanging three-shelf wooden corner cabinet made for "whatnots" I got at a yard sale. The shape and material are not as important as the elements you'll be using. Some kind of heart symbol should be included somewhere as it is essential to the concept.

Once you have the nicho you will be working with—whether a two-dimensional heart shape or a three-dimensional shadow-box format—you are ready to choose the elements that depict your love of the Sacred. What does "Sacred Heart" mean to you—what elements would you choose to illustrate your love for the Divine or your experience of the Divine's love for you? One of the most powerful art-making experiences I ever had, which I wrote about in *Crafting Calm*, involved an assignment to look through magazines for depictions of what the Divine meant to me. We were limited to choosing images from the particular magazines we had, and this inspired us to use interesting and creative interpretations. Some I found, for example, included a spider web adorned with crystalline dew and the wise, wrinkled face of a Native American elder.

For this project, you aren't limited—the only boundaries you face are finding representations that will fit the size of whatever field you're using as a background. All of the subjects covered in this book—love of romantic partners, friends and family, nature and humanity, self-love—might also be represented in some way as you choose the elements representing love of the Divine. A dried rosebud from your wedding bouquet, a button from your late father's shirt, a plastic-bead ring your child gave to you, a seashell from a special beach—these are examples of the spectrum of selections you might choose for your Sacred Heart Nicho.

As you select and sort, thinking back through your life as you choose the ingredients for your art, you may find yourself agreeing with Henry Drummond, who wrote: "You will find as you look back upon your life that the moments that stand out, the moments when you have really lived, are the moments when you have done things in a spirit of love."

Inner Inquiries for Journaling and Reflection

* When I think of the Divine—my love for the Divine and the Divine's love for me—what comes to mind? Memories of certain experiences? Particular scenes in nature? My child's face?

* How might seeing visual depictions of Divine love impact my day? What kind of ritual or remembrance—even if it's just to stop and look at it each morning— might I be able to use my Sacred Heart Nicho for, in order to remind myself of the abundance of Divine Love in my life?

> "Love is not an emotion. Love is your very existence."
> —SRI SRI RAVI SHANKAR

Conclusion

NO MATTER WHAT OUR FAVORITE CREATIVE PASTIME IS—painting, beading, collage making, or clay forming—there is at least one art form (and, hopefully, in this book you have found more) you can use as a way to "craft love." In this age where the darkest of human activities scroll across the bottom of our TV screens or at the top of our Internet pages, God knows we all need to experience more beauty in our lives, to feel a sense of belongingness and love, and to be reminded that, as the precocious teenager Anne Frank noted at a horrifying time in human history, "In spite of everything I still believe that people are really good at heart. . . . I can feel the sufferings of millions and yet, if I look up into the heavens, I think that it will all come out right, that this cruelty too will end, and that peace and tranquility will return again."

Crafting calm, crafting gratitude, and crafting love are ways to help us think that it will all come out right. They are ways to disavow the cruelty in the world and to help us experience peace and tranquility *now*, right here in the present moment. There is a wonderful quotation, a statement of faith, written by Martin Luther King Jr. usually incorrectly attributed to Martin Luther (there is no evidence of the aphorism used before 1944): "Even if I knew the world would end tomorrow, I would continue to plant my apple trees."

Employing our creative skills in any endeavor that could potentially outlast us—whether painting an apple tree, writing a poem about an apple tree, or planting one—is so much more than just the act itself. It becomes a stand we take: life and creation and beauty are worth something. In fact, they are worth everything.

At times, I have felt the purpose behind these three crafting books I've brought into the world has been a bit misunderstood. These were never intended to stand alone as encouragers of crafting-for-craft's-sake (of course there's nothing wrong with that), but rather to inspire crafting-for-God's sake—and I mean that literally. There is a transcendent state we can enter when making art, when crafting, that has been at the heart of all these explorations. This has always been about creating as a spiritual practice.

After *Crafting Calm* came out, I was given the opportunity by a website called Inspire-MeToday.com to write five hundred words on the wisdom I most wanted to share with the world. This is how I ended that essay:

> Paying attention to and expressing what is true, noble and right, pure and lovely and admirable, is a way of rising gently with each breath. It is not a superficial luxury in this world; it is an urgent necessity. It is being a light in the darkness, a protest against ugliness, a harmonic in dissonance, order in the midst of chaos. It is a political statement. It is a spiritual practice.
>
> It is a cause, and it is a calling. It is a line in the sand, a sign of determined resolution that proclaims that no matter what appearances or predictions might say, the Sacred does surround us. We are enfolded in the Holy. There is always something lovely to be found, always; and the search for it or deliberate creation of it is never frivolous. John Keats was right: "Beauty is Truth, Truth Beauty.

After I wrote that essay, I realized it was a personal manifesto of sorts—a declaration of some of my deepest feelings about what we're supposed to be doing on this often-crazy playground we call Life. I believe with every fiber of my being that one of the most profound purposes of life is to *create*. We were born to create—we were created by a Creator to contribute our own unique creations.

These three books—*Crafting Calm, Crafting Gratitude,* and *Crafting Love*—have been some of the ways I've tried to encourage that deliberate creation of beauty through using art and craft-making as a spiritual practice. Perhaps, more than ever before, as a species we need to discipline ourselves to build faith in the future by cultivating the creativity within each of us and by channeling our love in the direction of a world that works for all. In the words of Michael Bridge, "When our eyes see our hands doing the work of our hearts, the circle of Creation is completed inside us, the doors of our soul fly open and love steps forth to heal everything in sight."

Contributors

JEANINE BYERS is a spiritual coach, healer, and author of *Moon Healing for Mystics & Healers: How to Use the Phases of the Moon to Create the Life You Want* (published under a pen name). She helps women who feel spiritually disconnected to develop spiritual practices that deepen their connection to the goddess. Visit her website at dailyspiritualpractice.net.

HOLLY BYRAM has been creating art since she received her first set of finger paints as a child. Making art is something she jokingly says she must do, whether she wants to or not. Her work has evolved over the years through many different media: graphite drawing, colored pencil drawing, photography, oil painting, mosaic, and chain maille jewelry. At the heart of her expression lie the needs to explore and connect, and to say something about her human experiences that cannot be described in words. Contact Holly at holly.byram@gmail.com.

DONNA CALDWELL has served as senior minister of California's Unity of Castro Valley for more than twenty years. She is a proud great-grandmother of one daughter, two grandsons, and one set of great-grand-twin boys. She has many interests, including the sport of disk golf. Donna won a first-place prize in the 2012 Chick Flick Tournament in the Advanced Senior Grand Master Women's class. (Donna says that class sounds fancy, but just means that you are over sixty.) There are four generations of her family who play disk golf. The twins taught her a technique that helped her win the tournament. Donna can be reached at cvrev@aol.com.

WESTY FAISON attended Kenyon College, where he majored in fine art (studio). After studying with Frederick Franck in New York, he moved to the San Francisco Bay Area to pursue a career as a painter and decorative painting contractor (doing business as New Room Paint Design). He can be reached at westyfaison@gmail.com or (415) 318-6723.

SILVIA REYES GRADY, born in Mexico, grew up in the San Francisco Bay Area. Married for more than thirty years, she has two wonderful children and a granddaughter, has enjoyed a career as an educator, is a self-taught crafter and quilter, and a seeker of the Divine.

SUSAN HAMMACK is an artist, forager of truths, and glitter-licking mother of two living on the San Francisco Bay Area's coast. Her current interests are the nexus between art, healing, and spirituality particularly in the context of community building among women and volunteer work with youth. In her spare time you can find her walking on the beach with her dog Roxy, hunting for old vinyl with her husband and daughters, or taking the occasional accordion lesson. Connect with Susan at susansanellihammack.com.

JENNIFER A. MANTLE is a SoulCollage® facilitator, a Reiki Master, and a sign language interpreter. She offers regular classes in Reiki, SoulCollage® and art journaling in San Francisco, where she lives with her long-time partner and magical pup. She can be reached at phoenixwings73@gmail.com, her Etsy shop (adoreherdesigns.etsy.com), or through her website, SoulFullPlay.com.

RONNIE McCULLOGH describes her work this way: "Women provide the canvas for my current art, which is uncovering, midwifing, and awakening women to their innate and essential beauty and providing them with the tools to express this through the art of dress." She works in a partnership with Kathryn Heflin in a passionate business called Divine Style Makeovers. They have a website and Facebook presence under that name and Pinterest boards under pinterest.com/divine makeovers/. You can also email them at info@divinestylemakeovers.com or by phone at (707) 888-9808.

JUDY RANIERI, MA, is a legacy coach, wisdom keeper, joyologist, artist, author of *Take Time* and *Take Time for Joy,* and an explorer of life. Judy guides women to their inner wisdom using creativity and intuition to investigate the layers of knowing which we all have. Judy is a mother and grandmother, which brings her great joy and an abundance of gratitude. Contact Judy through her website: thewisdombox.com.

SUSYN REEVE is a best-selling author, master coach, interfaith minister, grandmother, GodMother, and elder, and is always, she says, feasting on life. Learn more at her website, SusynReeve.com.

JOAN RIVARD is a poet currently staying in San Francisco. If you're lucky, you might see her down south at Pasadena's Rose Bowl Flea Market—just look for The Cookie Lady in the "heaven-blue" skirt and hat with rainbow ribbons. She can be reached at joanrivard1776@gmail.com.

MELISSA RODGERS is a lifelong crafter, Certified Wellness Practitioner, and craft instructor. She lives in Northern California with her husband Paul, a professional wood-worker and partner in Artistic Economy, dedicated to the promotion and practice of creative living. At various times throughout the year they can be found traveling in their (handmade) gypsy wagon teaching and sharing traditional and creative arts. Melissa can be reached at artistic.economy@gmail.com.

DANNA SCHMIDT is a certified Life-Cycle Celebrant® and ceremonialist with Waypoint Ceremonies, and has been hosting workshops on creativity, spirituality, compassion, and ritual for several years. Truthing and daring others to kiss their creative bliss and own their self-sovereignty is how and why she puts her whole self into this hokey-pokey dance called life. She lives in Bellevue, Washington, and can be reached at soulcollage.com/danna-schmidt.

JENNIFER STOVER is an award-winning knitter, instructor, and designer who learned to knit in her early thirties from her mother. She actively participates in charity-based proj-ects and in-person and online social groups in Texas and Missouri. She currently resides in Saint Joseph, Missouri, with her husband, two children, and yarn stash that insulates their 120-year-old house nicely in the winter. She can be found on Ravelry as PhDaisy1.

DAWN TROOK is a performer, writer, and educator living in Merced, California, where she runs Project Big Top, a non-profit arts organization specializing in the development of original literary and performance works. She can often be seen as her alter-ego, Sweetie the Baker, who teaches science to kids through cooking workshops.

Acknowledgments

A BOOK ON CRAFTING LOVE WOULD NOT BE COMPLETE without expressing my loving appreciation to all those who contributed to the making of it. First thanks go to former Viva Editions publisher Brenda Knight for being the "common denominator" of all eight of my books and for her wonderful enthusiasm and support throughout the years. Thanks also to everyone on the talented team at Viva Editions for the great job they've done in the crafting of this book.

Heartfelt thanks to all those who I interviewed for this book and who contributed to it: Jeanine Byers, Holly Byram, Donna Caldwell, Westy Faison, Silvia Reyes Grady, Susan Hammack, Jennifer Mantle, Ronnie McCullough, Judy Ranieri, Susyn Reeve, Joan Rivard, Melissa Rodgers, Danna Schmidt, Jennifer Stover, and Dawn Trook. I have loved hearing your stories and am so grateful that our paths have crossed.

As always, I want to thank my congregants, family members, and friends, by whom I feel so lovingly supported. Lasting thanks go to Janice Farrell, my spiritual director for many years, who gave me such a loving gift when she affirmed that I seem to have a knack for creating spiritual practices out of the ingredients of everyday life. And I want to express my love here for my mother, Mary Jane Burruss Oman, who passed away during the writing of this book; and to my brother, Carl Oman, whose creativity has always inspired me.

Finally, to the two great loves of my life—my husband, Scott, and daughter, Chloe—thank you from the bottom of my heart for your patience, understanding, and support; for loving me enough to offer me the time and space to pursue projects like this one, which are so close to my heart.

Last but never least, eternal love and gratitude to Creative Spirit for the infinite parade of awe-producing wonders I enjoy every day. I am so blessed, and so grateful, and so in love with this journey we call life.

About the Author

The Reverend **MAGGIE OMAN SHANNON**, MA, is an ordained Unity minister, spiritual director, workshop and retreat facilitator, and author of seven previous books: *Prayers for Healing*; *The Way We Pray: Prayer Practices from Around the World*; *A String and a Prayer: How to Make and Use Prayer Beads* (co-author); *One God, Shared Hope*; *Prayers for Hope and Comfort*; *Crafting Calm: Projects and Practices for Creativity and Contemplation*; and *Crafting Gratitude: Creating and Celebrating Our Blessings with Hands and Heart*. In 2000, Oman Shannon founded The New Story, a coaching and consulting business focused on helping people create deeper meaning in their lives.

The former editor of three national magazines, including *The Saturday Evening Post,* Oman Shannon also served as Director of Marketing for the Institute of Noetic Sciences. Her writing has appeared in publications including *Utne Reader* and the *Huffington Post*, and her work has been featured in periodicals ranging from the *San Francisco Chronicle* to *Spirituality and Health* magazine. She has taught workshops at venues including California Pacific Medical Center's Institute for Health and Healing and Chautauqua Institution in Chautauqua, New York.

In addition to being a certified life coach, Oman Shannon completed the three-year training program of the Spiritual Directors Institute at Mercy Center in Burlingame, California. A graduate of Smith College, Oman Shannon also holds a master of arts degree in culture and spirituality from Holy Names University. A 2010 graduate of Manhattan's One Spirit Interfaith Seminary, she was ordained as a Unity minister in 2014.

Oman Shannon is the senior minister of Unity Spiritual Center of San Francisco, and has served as its spiritual leader since 2010. She also hosts "Creative Spirit," an hour-long weekly radio show on Unity.fm. She lives in San Francisco with her husband and teenage daughter, the place and the people she loves the most.

Resources

WEB SITES

Arts and Crafts as a Spiritual Practice

Abbeyofthehearts.com

Christine Valters Paintner's "monastery without walls," offering resources to nurture contemplative practice and creative expression

Artheals.org

The online resource of the Arts & Healing Network, celebrating the connection between art and healing

Crescendoh.com

Jenny Doh's blog, store, online classes, and other resources—because "art saves"

Explorefaith.org

A wonderful collection of articles on the spiritual life, including a "Meditate with Art" section

Janrichardson.com

The home of spiritual artist and writer Jan Richardson's various web offerings

Spiritualityandpractice.com

The motherlode of spiritual websites, featuring thousands of pages of resources gathered by Frederic and Mary Ann Brussat, including a section on gratitude

Stampington.com

The main home of Stampington magazines (see Magazines), which also features online tutorials and craft store

If you haven't yet joined **Pinterest.com,** you'll definitely want to sign up for a free account that will enable you to create virtual "pinboards" on every conceivable topic, including crafting and love. Look for me there at www.pinterest.com/revmaggie.

Also, please join my community page on **Facebook.com:** "Creating as a Spiritual Practice." You can also find me on **Instagram** (where I often post photos of my recent art and inspirations) at www.instagram.com/revmaggieo; and my **Etsy** store is www.mystic-mermaidstudio.etsy.com.

MAGAZINES

Stampington Studio publishes a large collection of magazines that may provide inspiration as you pursue crafting as a spiritual practice; a few in particular to check out are *Art Doll Quarterly, Art Journaling, Artful Blogging, HandCrafted, Life Images, Somerset Life,* and *Somerset Studio.*

BOOKS

General Interest

Art and Soul: 156 Ways to Free Your Creative Spirit by Pam Grout (Andrews McMeel Publishing, 2000)

The Complete Artist's Way: Creativity as a Spiritual Practice by Julia Cameron (Jeremy P. Tarcher/Penguin, 2007)

The Creative Call: An Artist's Response to the Way of the Spirit by Janice Elsheimer (Shaw Books, 2001)

Creative Spirituality: The Way of the Artist by Robert Wuthnow (University of California Press, 2001)

Everyday Spiritual Practice: Simple Pathways for Enriching Your Life edited by Scott W. Alexander (Skinner House Books, 1999)

Illuminations: Expressions of the Personal Spiritual Experience edited by Mark L. Tompkins and Jennifer McMahon (Celestial Arts, 2006)

Simple Abundance: A Daybook of Comfort and Joy by Sarah Ban Breathnach (Warner Books, 1995)

The Way We Pray: Prayer Practices from Around the World by Maggie Oman Shannon (Conari Press, 2001)

Creativity

The Artist Inside: A Spiritual Guide to Cultivating Your Creative Self by Tom Crockett (Broadway Books, 2000)

The Creative Habit: Learn It and Use It for Life by Twyla Tharp (Simon & Schuster, 2003)

Creative Is a Verb: If You're Alive, You're Creative by Patti Digh (Skirt!, 2011)

Creativity: Where the Divine and the Human Meet by Matthew Fox (Jeremy P. Tarcher/Penguin, 2004)

Freeing the Creative Spirit: Drawing on the Power of Art to Tap the Magic and Wisdom Within by Adriana Diaz (HarperSanFrancisco, 1992)

Learning by Heart: Teachings to Free the Creative Spirit by Corita Kent and Jan Steward (Bantam Books, 1992)

The Nine Muses: A Mythological Path to Creativity by Angeles Arrien (Jeremy P. Tarcher/ Penguin, 2000)

The Soul of Creativity: Insights into the Creative Process edited by Tona Pearce Myers (New World Library, 1999)

Soul Fire: Accessing Your Creativity by Thomas Ryan (Skylight Paths, 2008)

Stoking the Creative Fires: 9 Ways to Rekindle Passion and Imagination by Phil Cousineau (Conari Press, 2008)

Trust the Process: An Artist's Guide to Letting Go by Shaun McNiff (Shambala, 1998)

A Year of Creativity: A Seasonal Guide to New Awareness by Brenda Mallon (Andrews McMeel Publishing, 2003)

Creativity as a Form of Spiritual Practice

The Artist's Rule: Nurturing Your Creative Soul with Monastic Wisdom by Christine Valters Paintner (Sorin Books, 2011)

Crafting Calm: Projects and Practices for Creativity and Contemplation by Maggie Oman Shannon (Viva Editions, 2013)

Crafting Gratitude: Creating and Celebrating Our Blessings with Hands and Heart by Maggie Oman Shannon (Viva Editions, 2017)

Eyes of the Heart: Photography as a Christian Contemplative Practice by Christine Valters Paintner (Sorin Books, 2013)

The Knitting Sutra: Craft as a Spiritual Practice by Susan Gordon Lydon (HarperSanFrancisco, 1997)

The Knitting Way: A Guide to Spiritual Self-Discovery by Linda Skolnik and Janice Macdaniels (Skylight Paths, 2005)

Praying in Color: Drawing a New Path to God by Sybil MacBeth (Paraclete Press, 2007)

PHILOSOPHY AND CULTURE

The Art Abandonment Project: Create and Share Random Acts of Art by Michael deMeng and Andrea Matus deMeng (North Light Books, 2014)

Centering: In Pottery, Poetry, and the Person by M. C. Richards (Wesleyan University Press, 1976)

Concerning the Spiritual in Art by Wassily Kandinsky (Dover Publications, Inc., 1977)

The Courage to Create by Rollo May (Bantam Books, 1978)

Craft Activism: People, Ideas and Projects from the New Community of Handmade and How You Can Join In by Joan Tapper (Potter Craft, 2011)

The Creative Life: 7 Keys to Your Inner Genius by Eric Butterworth (Jeremy P. Tarcher/Putnam, 2001)

Desire to Inspire: Using Creative Passion to Transform the World by Christine Mason Miller (North Light Books, 2011)

Faith and Transformation: Votive Offerings and Amulets from the Alexander Girard Collection edited by Doris Francis (Museum of International Folk Art, 2007)

Image and Spirit: Finding Meaning in Visual Art by Karen Stone (Augsburg Books, 2003)

Making Is Connecting: The Social Meaning of Creativity, From DIY and Knitting to YouTube and Web 2.0 by David Gauntlett (Polity Press, 2011)

The Spirituality of Art by Lois Huey-Heck and Jim Kalnin (Northstone Publishing, 2006)

Walking on Water: Reflections on Faith and Art by Madeleine L'Engle (Harold Shaw Publishers, 1980)

A Way of Working: The Spiritual Dimension of Craft edited by D. M. Dooling (Parabola Books, 1986)

The Zen of Creativity: Cultivating Your Artistic Life by John Daido Loori (Ballantine Books, 2005)

CREATIVE EXERCISES

The Artist Inside: A Spiritual Guide to Cultivate Your Creative Self by Tom Crockett (Broadway Books, 2000)

Creating Change: The Arts as Catalyst for Spiritual Transformation edited by Keri K. Wehlander (CopperHouse, 2008)

Creativity and Divine Surprise: Finding the Place of Your Resurrection by Karla M. Kincannon (Upper Room Books, 2005)

Cultivating Your Creative Life: Exercises, Activities & Inspiration for Finding Balance, Beauty & Success as an Artist by Alena Hennessy (Quarry Books, 2012)

Making Things: A Book of Days for the Creative Spirit by Janet Carija Brandt (Martingale & Co., 2005)

Spirit Taking Form: Making a Spiritual Practice of Making Art by Nancy Azara (Red Wheel, 2002)

Spiritual Doodles & Mental Leapfrogs: A Playbook for Unleashing Spiritual Self-Expression by Katherine Q. Revoir (Red Wheel/Weiser, 2002)

Windows into the Soul: Art as Spiritual Expression by Michael Sullivan (Morehouse Publishing, 2006)

HEALING/THERAPEUTIC APPLICATIONS

Art Saves: Stories, Inspiration and Prompts Sharing the Power of Art by Jenny Doh (North Light Books, 2011)

Awakening the Creative Spirit: Bringing the Arts to Spiritual Direction by Christine Valters Paintner and Betsey Beckman (Morehouse Publishing, 2010)

Craft to Heal: Soothing Your Soul with Sewing, Painting, and Other Pastimes by Nancy Monson (Hats Off Books, 2011)

The Creative Connection: Expressive Arts as Healing by Natalie Rogers (Science & Behavior Books, Inc., 1993)

Healing with the Arts: A 12-Week Program to Heal Yourself and Your Community by Michael Samuels, MD, and Mary Rockwood Lane, RN, PhD (Atria Books/Beyond Words, 2013)

Illuminations: The Healing Image by Madeline McMurray (Wingbow Press, 1988)

The Soul's Palette: Drawing on Art's Transformative Powers for Health and Well-Being by Cathy A. Malchiodi (Shambala, 2002)

Spirituality and Art Therapy: Living the Connection edited by Mimi Farrelly-Hansen (Jessica Kingsley Publishers, 2001)

TECHNIQUE / HOW-TO

A String and a Prayer: How to Make and Use Prayer Beads by Eleanor Wiley and Maggie Oman Shannon (Red Wheel/Weiser, 2002)

A String of Expression: Techniques for Transforming Art and Life into Jewelry by June Roman (North Light Books, 2010)

Beading—The Creative Spirit: Finding Your Sacred Center through the Art of Beadwork by Rev. Wendy Ellsworth (Skylight Paths, 2009)

Collage for the Soul: Expressing Hopes and Dreams Through Art by Holly Harrison & Paula Grasdal (Rockport Publishers, Inc., 2003)

Contemplative Crochet: A Hands-On Guide for Interlocking Faith and Craft by Cindy Crandall-Frazier (Skylight Paths, 2008)

Inspiritu Jewelry: Earrings, Bracelets, and Necklaces for the Mind, Body, and Spirit by Marie French (North Light Books, 2011)

The Painting Path: Embodying Spiritual Discovery through Yoga, Brush and Color by Linda Novick (Skylight Paths, 2007)

The Quilting Path: A Guide to Spiritual Discovery through Fabric, Thread and Kabbalah by Louise Silk (Skylight Paths, 2006)

The Soulwork of Clay: A Hands-on Approach to Spirituality by Marjory Zoet Bankson (Skylight Paths, 2008)

Spirit Crafts by Cheryl Owen (CLB International, 1997)

Index